BASIC

Grammar in Context

SANDRA N. ELBAUM

JUDI PEMÁN

THOMSON

HEINLE

United States • Australia • Canada • Mexico • Singapore • Spain • United Kingdom

Grammar in Context, Basic

SANDRA N. ELBAUM

JUDI PEMÁN

Publisher, Adult & Academic: *James W. Brown*
Senior Acquisitions Editor, Adult & Academic:
Sherrise Roehr
Director of Product Development: *Anita Raducanu*
Director of Marketing: *Amy Mabley*
Marketing Manager: *Laura Needham*
Senior Print Buyer: *Mary Beth Hennebury*
Development Editor: *Charlotte Sturdy*

Compositor: *Nesbitt Graphics, Inc.*
Project Manager: *Julie DeSilva*
Photo Researcher: *Connie Gardner*
Illustrators: *James Edwards, Gershom Griffith,*
Keith Lesko, Meredith Morgan, and Len Shalansky
Interior Designer: *Jerilyn Bockorick*
Cover Designer: *Joseph Sherman*
Printer: *Quebecor World*

Cover Image: © Jerry Emmons

Printed in the United States of America.
1 2 3 4 5 6 7 8 9 10   09 08 07 06

For more information contact Thomson Heinle,
25 Thomson Place, Boston, Massachusetts 02210
USA, or you can visit our Internet site at
elt.thomson.com

ISBN: 1-4130-0638-8
International Student Edition: 1-4130-1534-4

Library of Congress Control Number: 2006900241

Photo Credits:

1, left James Leynse/CORBIS, *right* Adrian Peacock/Picturequest;
7, Catherine Karnow/CORBIS; *12, quarter* David Young Wolff/
PhotoEdit, *dime* Jonathan Nourock/PhotoEdit, *dollar bill* Joseph
Sohm/The Image Works, *penny* Bill Aron/PhotoEdit; *14,* Susan
Van Etten/PhotoEdit; *17,* Tim Boyle/Getty Images; *23, top*
Howard Dracht/The Image Works, *center* Martin Gerten/Getty
Images, *bottom* Bob Daemmrich/The ImageWorks; *33,* Royalty
Free/CORBIS; *38,* David M. Grossman/The Image Works; *40,*
Michael Newman/PhotoEdit; *43, left* Andrew Holbrooke/The
Image Works, *right* John Griffin/The Image Works; *44, card*
David Young Wolf/PhotoEdit, *license* Clayton Sharrard/PhotoEdit,
passport Index Open, *marriage certificate* Clayton Sharrard/
PhotoEdit, *college ID* David Barber/PhotoEdit; *48,* Jeff Greenberg/
PhotoEdit; *54,* MAK/The Image Works; *57, left* Paul Barton/
CORBIS, Michael Newman/PhotoEdit, *right* Royalty Free/CORBIS;
67, Ted Horowitz/CORBIS; *73,* Lindsey Hebbard/CORBIS; *74,*
Cathrine Wessel/CORBIS; *86,* Rudi von Briel/PhotoEdit; *89 left*
Ryan McVay/Getty Images, *right* Rob and SAS/CORBIS; *111, left*
Bob Daemmrich/PhotoEdit; *right* Will and Deni McIntyre/COR-
BIS, *117,* Charles Gupton/CORBIS; *124,* RNT Productions/ COR-
BIS; *131,* Dave Nagel/Getty Images; *135, left* Jeff Zaruka/CORBIS,
right James Leynse/CORBIS; *142,* Amy Etra/PhotoEdit; *143,*
Ronnie Kaufman/CORBIS; *152,* Jeff Greenberg/PhotoEdit; *155,*
Tim Boyle/Getty Images; *159,* Dennis MacDonald/PhotoEdit; *163,*
left Rudi von Briel/PhotoEdit, *right* Ryan McVay/Getty Images;
164, David Young Wolff/PhotoEdit; *166,* Tony Freeman/
PhotoEdit; *172,* Jeff Greenberg/PhotoEdit; *182,* Jim West/Alamy;
185, left Network Production/The Image Works, *right* Larry
Kolvoco/The Image Works; *198,* Tom and Dee Ann
McCarthy/CORBIS; *201,* Michael Newman/PhotoEdit; *203,* David
Young Wolff/PhotoEdit; *206,* Myrleen Cate Ferguson/PhotoEdit;
209, left Don Mason/CORBIS, *right* Colin Young Wolff/PhotoEdit;
212, Bob Mahoney/The Image Works; *215,* Christina
Kennedy/PhotoEdit; *217,* Bob Daemmrich/The Image Works; *219,*
Mark Gamba/CORBIS; *222,* Mark Richard/PhotoEdit; *231, left*
Left Lane Productions/CORBIS, *right* Michael
Newman/PhotoEdit; *232, left* FRISHLING STEVEN E/CORBIS
SYGMA, *right* Ed Bock/CORBIS; *246,* David Young
Wolff/PhotoEdit; *256, left* Reuters/CORBIS, *right* FogStock
LLC/IndexStock Imagery RF; *257, child* Ellen Senisi/The Image
Works, *building house* Jim West/The Image Works, *helping with
groceries* Tony Freeman/PhotoEdit; *273,* Bob Daemmrich/The
Image Works; *280* Ed Bock/CORBIS; *276,* A. Ramey/PhotoEdit

Contents

Unit 3

Unit 4

GRAMMAR The Simple Present Tense; Frequency Words

CONTEXT American Lifestyles

Unit 5

GRAMMAR Modal Verbs: *Can, Should, Have To*

CONTEXT Driving

Unit 6

GRAMMAR *Must* and *Have To*; Noncount Nouns; Quantity Expressions

CONTEXT School

Unit 7

GRAMMAR Prepositions; *There Is/There Are*

CONTEXT Shopping

Unit 8

GRAMMAR The Present Continuous Tense; Time Expressions

CONTEXT Errands

Unit 11

GRAMMAR   The Past Tense of *Be*; Regular Verbs in the Simple Past Tense; Irregular Verbs in the Past Tense; Time Expressions with the Past Tense

CONTEXT   Getting a Job

Unit 12

GRAMMAR   Verb Review: Simple Present Tense; Present Continuous Tense; Future Tense; Simple Past Tense; Modal Verbs: *Can, Should, Must, Have To*

CONTEXT   Giving Back

Appendices

For

Cassia, Gentille, Chimene, Joseph and Joy

Acknowledgments

Many thanks to Dennis Hogan, Jim Brown, Sherrise Roehr, and Sally Giangrande from Thomson Heinle for their ongoing support of the *Grammar in Context* series. We would especially like to thank our editor, Charlotte Sturdy, for her keen eye to detail and invaluable suggestions.

And many thanks to our students at Truman College, who have increased our understanding of our own language and taught us to see life from another point of view. By sharing their observations, questions, and life stories, they have enriched our lives enormously.

Heinle would like to thank the following reviewers:

Lisa DiPaolo
Sierra College
Rocklin, CA

Maha Edlbi
Sierra College
Rocklin,CA

Kathy Krokar
City College of Chicago/Harry Truman
Chicago, IL

Robert Wachman
Yuba College
Yuba City, CA

Joan Amore
Triton College
River Grove, IL

Herbert Pierson
St. John's University
Queens, NY

The *Grammar in Context* Series

Students learn more, remember more, and use language more effectively when they learn grammar in context.

Learning a language through meaningful themes and practicing it in a contextualized setting promote both linguistic and cognitive development. In **Grammar in Context**, grammar is presented in interesting and culturally informative readings, and the language and context are subsequently practiced throughout the chapter.

New to this edition:

- **New and updated readings** on current American topics such as Instant Messaging and eBay.
- **Updated grammar charts** that now include essential language notes.
- **Updated exercises and activities** that provide contextualized practice using a variety of exercise types, as well as additional practice for more difficult structures.
- **New lower-level** *Grammar in Context Basic* for beginning level students.
- **New wrap-around Teacher's Annotated Edition** with page-by-page, point-of-use teaching suggestions.
- **Expanded Assessment CD-ROM** with ExamView® Pro Test Generator now contains more questions types and assessment options to easily allow teachers to create tests and quizzes.

Distinctive Features of the *Grammar in Context* Series:

Students are prepared for academic assignments and everyday language tasks.

Discussions, readings, compositions, and exercises involving higher-level critical thinking skills develop overall language and communication skills.

Students expand their knowledge of American topics and culture.

The readings in **Grammar in Context** help students gain insight into and enrich their knowledge of American culture and history. Students have ample exposure to the practicalities of American life, such as getting a driver's license, applying for a Social Security card, writing a resume, dealing with telemarketers, and getting student internships. Their new knowledge helps them adapt to everyday life in the U.S.

Students learn to use their new skills to communicate.

The exercises and Expansion Activities in **Grammar in Context** help students learn English while practicing their reading, writing, listening, and speaking skills. Students work together in pairs or groups to find more information about topics and about each other, to make presentations, to play games, and to role-play. Their confidence in using English increases, as does their ability to communicate effectively.

Welcome to **Grammar in Context Basic**

Students learn more, remember more and use language more effectively when they learn grammar in context.

Grammar in Context Basic connects grammar with rich, American cultural content, providing learners of English with a useful and meaningful knowledge base.

Readings and Dialogues on topics such as the supermarket, finding a new car, or moving to a new home present and illustrate the grammatical structure in an informative and meaningful context.

Vocabulary in Context boxes include new and important words to help students build their vocabulary base and increase their ability to use new words in context.

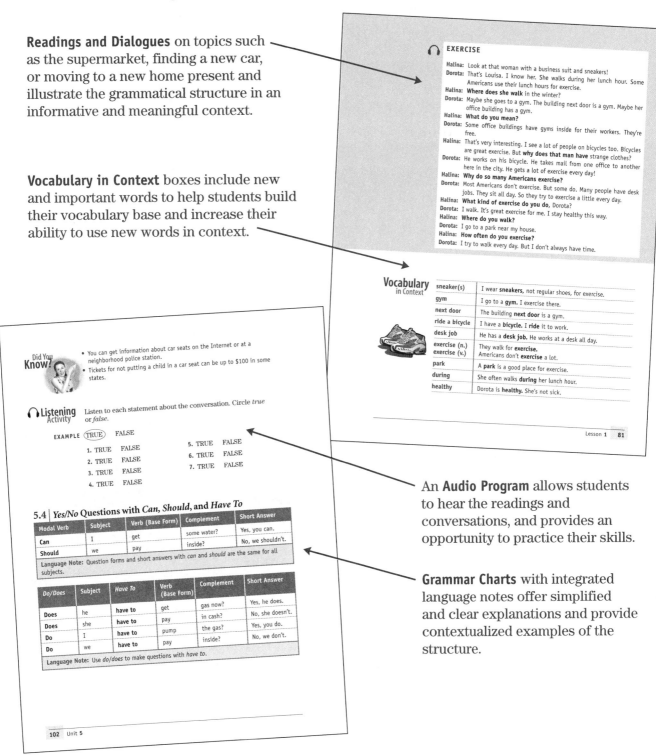

An **Audio Program** allows students to hear the readings and conversations, and provides an opportunity to practice their skills.

Grammar Charts with integrated language notes offer simplified and clear explanations and provide contextualized examples of the structure.

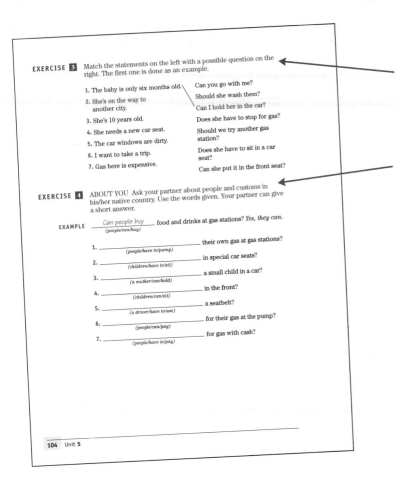

EXERCISE **3** Match the statements on the left with a possible question on the right. The first one is done as an example.

1. The baby is only six months old.
2. She's on the way to another city.
3. She's 10 years old.
4. She needs a new car seat.
5. The car windows are dirty.
6. I want to take a trip.
7. Gas here is expensive.

Can you go with me?
Should she wash them?
Can I hold her in the car?
Does she have to stop for gas?
Should we try another gas station?
Does she have to sit in a car seat?
Can she put it in the front seat?

EXERCISE **4** ABOUT YOU Ask your partner about people and customs in his/her native country. Use the words given. Your partner can give a short answer.

EXAMPLE <u>Can people buy</u> food and drinks at gas stations? *Yes, they can.*
         (people/can/buy)

1. _____ their own gas at gas stations?
   (people/have to/pump)
2. _____ in special car seats?
   (children/have to/sit)
3. _____ a small child in a car?
   (a mother/can/hold)
4. _____ in the front?
   (children/can/sit)
5. _____ a seatbelt?
   (a driver/have to/use)
6. _____ for their gas at the pump?
   (people/can/pay)
7. _____ for gas with cash?
   (people/have to/pay)

104 Unit **5**

A variety of contextualized activities keeps the classroom lively and targets different learning styles.

About You activities provide for language personalization and communication opportunities.

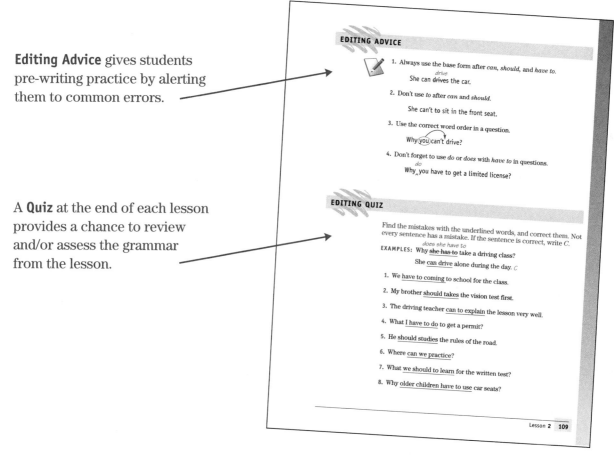

EDITING ADVICE

1. Always use the base form after *can*, *should*, and *have to*.
   She can ~~drives~~ drive the car.

2. Don't use *to* after *can* and *should*.
   She can't ~~to~~ sit in the front seat.

3. Use the correct word order in a question.
   Why you can't drive?

4. Don't forget to use *do* or *does* with *have to* in questions.
   Why do you have to get a limited license?

EDITING QUIZ

Find the mistakes with the underlined words, and correct them. Not every sentence has a mistake. If the sentence is correct, write C.

EXAMPLES: Why <u>she has to</u> take a driving class? *does she have to*
          She <u>can drive</u> alone during the day. *C*

1. We <u>have to coming</u> to school for the class.
2. My brother <u>should takes</u> the vision test first.
3. The driving teacher <u>can to explain</u> the lesson very well.
4. What <u>I have to do</u> to get a permit?
5. He <u>should studies</u> the rules of the road.
6. Where <u>can we practice</u>?
7. What <u>we should to learn</u> for the written test?
8. Why <u>older children have to use</u> car seats?

Lesson **2** **109**

Editing Advice gives students pre-writing practice by alerting them to common errors.

A **Quiz** at the end of each lesson provides a chance to review and/or assess the grammar from the lesson.

xiv Welcome to Grammar in Context **Basic**

A **Learner's Log** encourages students to reflect on what they have learned and to look for more information if needed.

Expansion Activities provide opportunities for students to interact with one another and with native speakers outside of class to further develop their speaking and writing skills.

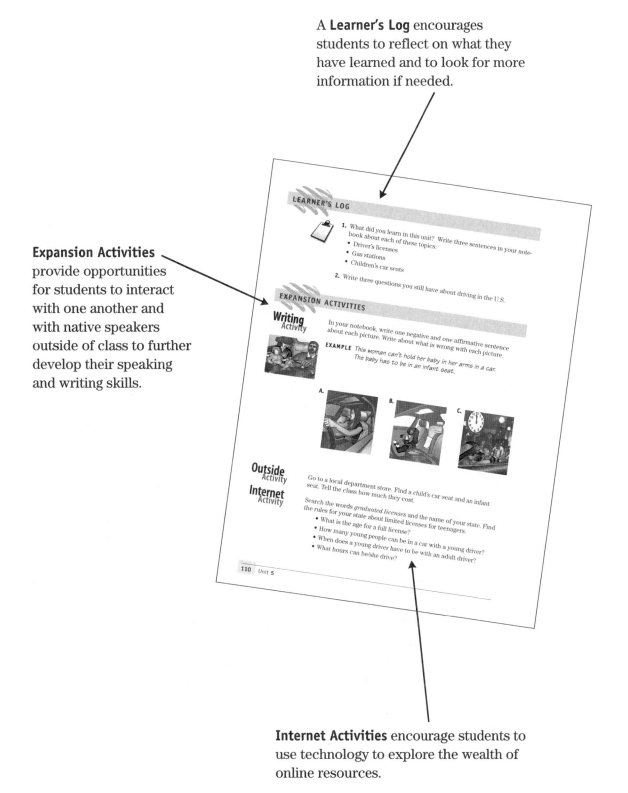

LEARNER'S LOG

1. What did you learn in this unit? Write three sentences in your notebook about each of these topics:
   • Driver's licenses
   • Gas stations
   • Children's car seats

2. Write three questions you still have about driving in the U.S.

EXPANSION ACTIVITIES

Writing Activity

In your notebook, write one negative and one affirmative sentence about each picture. Write about what is wrong with each picture.

EXAMPLE This woman can't hold her baby in her arms in a car. The baby has to be in an infant seat.

A.

B.

C.

Outside Activity

Go to a local department store. Find a child's car seat and an infant seat. Tell the class how much they cost.

Internet Activity

Search the words *graduated licenses* and the name of your state. Find the rules for your state about limited licenses for teenagers.
• What is the age for a full license?
• How many young people can be in a car with a young driver?
• When does a young driver have to be with an adult driver?
• What hours can he/she drive?

110   Unit 5

Internet Activities encourage students to use technology to explore the wealth of online resources.

About this book:

Grammar in Context Basic, an all-new addition to the *Grammar in Context* series, is a beginning level text book for low level ESL students who have had some exposure to English. Each unit continues the American culture theme that is the focus of the *Grammar in Context* series, but does so in a more personal way through the use of recurring characters. *Grammar in Context Basic* introduces Simon and Dorota, two immigrant Americans who help other immigrants adjust to life in the U.S. Throughout the book, Simon and Dorota take their new friends to the places that are part of everyday American life and help them learn to do things that will make their new lives easier: buy a used car, interview for a job, go shopping, fill out applications, and more.

The charts and exercises are similar to those found in the rest of the series but are designed with the beginning learner in mind. New to this level are Vocabulary in Context boxes, Listening Activities, and a Learner's Log, all features that are created to help beginning learners increase their overall language skills.

There are 12 Units (topically and structurally thematic), and each Unit has from two to four Lessons within. Each Lesson starts with a picture to introduce a reading (a narrative or a conversation), a Vocabulary in Context box that highlights unfamiliar or useful words in the reading, and a Listening Activity to practice comprehension. Clear and concise grammar charts highlight target structures using sentences from the Lesson theme. The exercises that follow also refer to the theme of the Lesson. Each Unit ends with Editing Advice reviewing the grammar in the Lesson, a Quiz, a Learner's Log, Expansion Activities, and Internet Activities. Each Unit should take approximately three to four classroom hours, depending on the complexity of the structure and the needs of your students.

At the end of *Grammar in Context Basic*, students should have a good introduction to the most common grammatical structures of the English language. Students will then be ready for more in-depth study and practice of each structure as found in *Grammar in Context* Books 1, 2, and 3.

Enjoy using *Grammar in Context Basic*!

Sandy and Judi

Grammar in Context Student Book Supplements

Audio Program
- Audio CDs and Audio Tapes allow students to listen to every reading in the book and hear Listening Activity questions.

More Grammar Practice Workbooks
- Workbooks can be used with *Grammar in Context* or any skills text to learn and review the essential grammar.
- Great for in-class practice or homework.
- Includes practice on all grammar points in *Grammar in Context*.

Teacher's Annotated Edition
- New component offers page-by-page answers and teaching suggestions.

Assessment CD-ROM with ExamView® Pro Test Generator
- Test Generator allows teachers to create tests and quizzes quickly and easily.

Interactive CD-ROM
- CD-ROM allows for supplemental interactive practice on grammar points from *Grammar in Context*.

Split Editions
- Split Editions for Books 1, 2, 3 provide options for short courses.

Instructional Video/DVD
- Video offers teaching suggestions and advice on how to use *Grammar in Context*.

Web Site
- Web site gives access to additional activities and promotes the use of the Internet.

It is nice to meet you!

Dorota Marta Simon Amy Ed Tina Peter with Anna Halina

Lisa Maya Victor Shafia & her husband Sue Rick Val Rhonda Matt Elsa

GRAMMAR

Subject Pronouns
Be
Contractions
Singular and Plural
This/That/These/Those
Adjectives
Expressions with *It*

CONTEXT

Welcome to the U.S.

GRAMMAR

Subject Pronouns
Forms of *Be*

CONTEXT

We Are Here to Help

Before You Read

Circle *yes* or *no*.

1. Many things are new for me in this country.   YES   NO
2. People help me with new things.   YES   NO

WE ARE HERE TO HELP

Dorota: Welcome! My name **is** Dorota. I **am** from Poland, but I **am** a citizen of the U.S. now. My first language **is** Polish. This **is** Simon. He **is** from Mexico. We **are** here to help you.

Simon: Hi. My name **is** Simon. I **am** from Mexico, but I **am** a citizen now. Spanish **is** my first language. We **are** both here to help you.

Dorota: You **are** new in this country. You **are** immigrants. Life **is** different here. Many things **are** different for you—the supermarket **is** different, the Laundromat **is** different, the doctor's office **is** different, and the bank **is** different. Everything **is** new for you. Maybe you **are** confused.

Simon: We **are** here to help you in new places. The Laundromat and supermarket **are** the first places to go.

They **are** helpful.

Vocabulary in Context

citizen	Dorota is a **citizen** of the United States.
both	Dorota and Simon are **both** here to help.
immigrant	I am from Colombia. I am new to the U.S. I am an **immigrant**.
life	**Life** in the U.S. is new for me.
supermarket	We buy food in a **supermarket**.
Laundromat	The **Laundromat** is a place to wash clothes.
different	The supermarket in the U.S. is **different**.
bank	He needs money. He is at the **bank**.
everything	**Everything** is new—the bank, the supermarket, and the Laundromat.
helpful	Dorota and Simon are **helpful**.
confused	I am new here. Everything is different. I'm **confused**.

Many agencies and volunteers help immigrants.

Listening Activity

Listen to the sentences about the story and picture. Circle *true* or *false*.

EXAMPLE TRUE (FALSE)

1. TRUE   FALSE
2. TRUE   FALSE
3. TRUE   FALSE
4. TRUE   FALSE
5. TRUE   FALSE
6. TRUE   FALSE

1.1 | Subject Pronouns

EXERCISE 1 Fill in the blanks with the correct subject pronoun.

EXAMPLE __*You*__ are immigrants.

1. Dorota is from Poland. _____ is here to help.

2. _____ am new to this country.

3. Simon is from Mexico. _____ is from Mexico City.

4. You and I are new. _____ are confused.

5. The bank is near my house. _____ is big.

6. Simon and Dorota are citizens now. _____ are helpful.

7. Halina: Thank you for your help.

   Simon: _____ are welcome.

1.2 | Forms of *Be*

Subject	Form of *Be*	Complement
I	**am**	a citizen.
The supermarket It Dorota She Simon He	**is**	different. big. from Poland. helpful. from Mexico. an American citizen.
We You Dorota and Simon They	**are**	here to help. new here. American citizens. helpful.

EXERCISE 2 Fill in the missing words: *am, is,* or *are.*

EXAMPLE The Laundromat __*is*__ different.

1. You _____ new here.

2. We _____ here to help you.

3. He _____ confused.

4. Some things _____ new.

5. I _____ a citizen now.

6. They _____ helpful.

7. She _____ from Poland.

EXERCISE 3 *Conversation:* Dorota and Halina are talking. Fill in the blanks with the correct form of *be*.

Dorota: You _____ new.
                     (1)

Halina: Yes. I _____ from Poland.
                     (2)

Dorota: I _____ from Poland too. I _____ an
               (3)   *(4)*

American citizen now. I _____ here to help you. Simon
                                 (5)

_____ here to help you too. He _____ from
     (6)   *(7)*

Mexico.

Halina: Many things _____ new for me.
                            (8)

Dorota: Yes. Life _____
                   (9)

different here. But we

_____ both here
    (10)

to help you.

Halina: Thank you.

EXERCISE 4 ABOUT YOU Check the items that are true for you.

EXAMPLE _____✓_____ I am new to the U.S.

_____ I am a citizen of the U.S.

1. _____ I am new to the U.S.

2. _____ I am new at this school.

3. _____ Life is different in a new country.

4. _____ I am confused about life in the U.S.

5. _____ I am a citizen of the U.S.

6. _____ I am an immigrant.

7. _____ Americans are helpful.

8. _____ I am from Mexico.

9. _____ Spanish is my native language.

10. _____ My family is in the U.S.

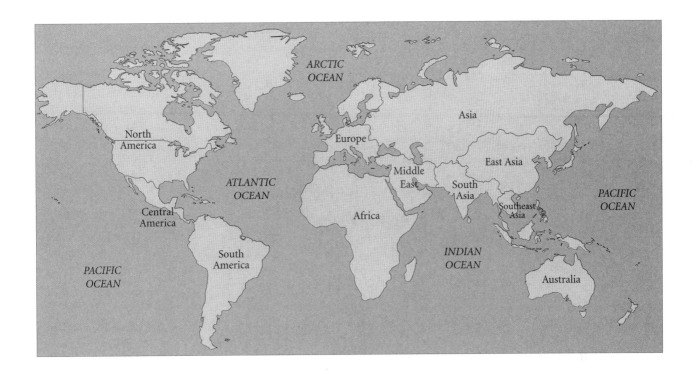

EXERCISE 5 ABOUT YOU Fill in the blanks.

EXAMPLE I am a citizen of _____ *Peru* _____.

1. My name is _____.
2. I am from _____.
3. My country is _____.
4. I am confused about _____.
5. _____ is helpful in my life here.
6. _____ is different for me.

LESSON 2

GRAMMAR

Contractions (Short Forms)
Singular and Plural
This/That/These/Those

CONTEXT

Help at the Laundromat

Before You Read

Circle *yes* or *no*.

1. I use the Laundromat. YES   NO

2. I wash some things by hand. YES   NO

HELP AT THE LAUNDROMAT

Dorota and a new immigrant, Shafia, are at the Laundromat.

Dorota: **We're** at the Laundromat.

Shafia: The **Laundromat's** new for me. **I'm** confused.

Dorota: Don't worry. **We're** together. **I'm** here to help you.

Shafia: Thanks. My clothes are dirty.

Dorota: These are the washing machines. The small machines are for small items—clothes, towels, and sheets. Those big machines are for big items, like blankets. Coins are necessary for the machines.

Shafia: Those machines are different.

Dorota: Yes. **They're** dryers.

Shafia: **It's** hot inside the Laundromat.

Dorota: **You're** right.

Shafia: **It's** easy to wash clothes in a Laundromat.

Dorota: Yes, it is.

Shafia: These two washers are empty. **I'm** ready to wash my clothes.

don't worry	**Don't worry.** I'm here to help you.
together	We're **together**.
right	**A:** It's hot here. **B:** Yes, you're **right**.
item(s)	These machines are for small **items**.
clothes	These are my **clothes**.
towel(s)	The **towels** are clean.
sheet(s)	The **sheets** are clean.
blanket(s)	The **blankets** are big.
coin(s)	**Coins** are necessary for the machines.
washing machine(s)	Those are the **washing machines**.
dryer(s)	Those are the **dryers**.
empty	The dryer is **empty**.
clean	My clothes are **clean** now.
dirty	Your clothes are **dirty**.

Clothes have washing instructions in the label.

hand wash only,
cold water

Listening Activity Listen to the sentences about the story. Circle *true* or *false*.

EXAMPLE (TRUE) FALSE

1. TRUE FALSE   4. TRUE FALSE

2. TRUE FALSE   5. TRUE FALSE

3. TRUE FALSE

1.3 | Contractions (Short Forms)

Long Form		Contraction (Short Form)	Examples
I am	→	I'm	**I'm** here to help.
She is	→	She's	**She's** from Poland.
He is	→	He's	**He's** from Mexico.
It is	→	It's	**It's** hot in here.
Life is	→	Life's	**Life's** different.
Everything is	→	Everything's	**Everything's** new.
Dorota is	→	Dorota's	**Dorota's** from Poland.
The Laundromat is	→	The Laundromat's	The **Laundromat's** hot.
You are	→	You're	**You're** very helpful.
We are	→	We're	**We're** together.
They are	→	They're	**They're** dryers.
Language Note: Do not use a contraction (short form) with a plural noun + **are**. The **dryers are** empty.			

EXERCISE 1 Write the contraction.

EXAMPLE (I am) _____ I'm _____ new here.

1. (Simon is) _____ from Mexico.

2. (He is) _____ a citizen of the U.S. now.

3. (Dorota is) _____ from Poland.

4. (She is) _____ a citizen too.

5. (They are) _____ both very helpful.

6. (The Laundromat is) _____ big.

7. (It is) _____ hot in the Laundromat.

8. (You are) _____ confused.

9. (I am) _____ confused too.

10. (We are) _____ both confused.

EXERCISE 2 Maria and Sara are new immigrants. This is their conversation. Fill in the blanks to complete the contraction.

Maria: I'_m___ from Mexico. ___You___ 're from Mexico
          (example)   (example)

too, right?

Sara: No. _____'m from Peru. It'_____ in South America.
              (1)   (2)

I'_____ in the U.S. with my parents. They'_____ old.
  (3)   (4)

Maria: _____'m here alone. I'_____ confused.
           (5)   (6)

Sara: We'_____ both confused. Many things are new here.
             (7)

Maria: Life'_____ different here. The bank'_____
                (8)   (9)

new for me. The school'_____ new for me.
                       (10)

Sara: Simon and Dorota are citizens now. Simon'_____ from
                                                   (11)

Mexico. _____'s helpful. Dorota'_____ from Poland.
        (12)   (13)

_____'s helpful too.
(14)

Maria: _____'re both very helpful to new immigrants.
           (15)

Sara: You'_____ right.
              (16)

1.4 | Singular and Plural

Singular means one. *Plural* means more than one. A plural noun usually ends in *-s*.

Singular	Plural
one machine	five machine**s**
one coin	six coin**s**
one towel	three towel**s**
one blanket	two blanket**s**

EXERCISE **3** Write the plural form of the words.

EXAMPLE sheet ___*sheets*___

1. quarter _____
2. dime _____
3. dryer _____
4. cent _____
5. machine _____
6. towel _____
7. item _____

8. blanket _____
9. coin _____
10. dollar _____

1.5 | *This, That, These, Those*

	Singular		Plural	
Near →	**This** is a Laundromat.		**These** are quarters.	
Not near ⟶	**That** is a big machine.		**Those** are the dryers.	

Language Note: Only *that is* has a short form—*that's.*
   That's a big machine.
Pronunciation Note: It's hard for many students to hear the difference between *this* and *these.* Listen to your teacher pronounce the sentences above.

EXERCISE 4 Fill in the blanks with *this is*, *that's*, *these are*, or *those are*.

EXAMPLE ___That's___ the coin machine.

 1. _____ a dollar.

 2. _____ coins.

 3. _____ quarters.

4. _____ the big washing machines.

 5. _____ a hot Laundromat.

 6. _____ dryers.

EXERCISE 5 Circle the correct word.

EXAMPLE The (*sheet*/(sheets)) are white.

1. The blankets (*is/are*) big.
2. (*These/This*) are the dryers.
3. (*They're/They*) hot.
4. (*Quarter/Quarters*) are necessary for the machine.
5. (*That/Those*) machines are empty.

GRAMMAR

Negative Forms of the Verb *Be*
Adjectives
Expressions with *It*
Singular and Plural

CONTEXT

Help at the Supermarket

Before You Read

Circle *yes* or *no*.

1. American supermarkets are confusing. YES   NO

2. Prices are the same in every supermarket. YES   NO

HELP AT THE SUPERMARKET

Dorota: We're at the supermarket now. It's early. The supermarket **isn't** crowded. The parking lot**'s not** crowded.

Halina: This is my first time in an American supermarket. I**'m not** sure what to do.

Dorota: I'm here to help you.

Halina: Thanks. The prices **aren't** on the products.

Dorota: The prices are on the shelves, under the products. A code is on each package.

Dorota: Prices **aren't** the same every week. Some things are on sale each week. Look—bananas are on sale this week. They're usually 69¢ a pound. This week they**'re not** 69¢ a pound. They're 29¢ a pound.

Halina: Look! These cookies are free.

Dorota: The samples are free, but the bags of cookies **aren't**.

Dorota: We're finished. This line is empty.

Halina: The cashier**'s not** here.

Dorota: It's an automatic checkout.

 **Vocabulary** in Context

early	It's 8 a.m. It's **early**.
crowded	The store is empty. It isn't **crowded**.
sure	I'm not **sure** what to do.
price	The **price** is 29¢ a pound.
product(s)	The supermarket has many **products**.
shelf/shelves	The prices are on the **shelves**.
code	A **code** is on each product.
package(s)	The cookies are in **packages**.
the same	Prices aren't **the same** every week.
on sale	Bananas are **on sale** this week.
pound(s)	Americans use **pounds**, not kilograms.
free	The bags of cookies are not **free**.
sample(s)	The **samples** are free.
cashier(s)	The **cashiers** are in the front of the store.
automatic checkout	You can use the **automatic checkout**.

- You can use cash, a check, a debit card, or a credit card to shop at the supermarket.
- Supermarkets produce papers that show all the sale items for the week.

 **Listening Activity**

Listen to the sentences about the story and pictures. Circle *true* or *false*.

EXAMPLE   TRUE   (FALSE)

1. TRUE	FALSE		4. TRUE	FALSE
2. TRUE	FALSE		5. TRUE	FALSE
3. TRUE	FALSE		6. TRUE	FALSE

1.6 | Negative Forms of the Verb *Be*

Negative Long Form	Negative Short Form	Negative Short Form
I am not sure.	**I'm not** sure.	
You are not serious.	**You're not** serious.	**You aren't** serious.
She is not sure. **He is not** at home. **The store is not** small. **It is not** crowded.	**She's not** sure. **He's not** at home. **The store's not** small. **It's not** crowded.	**She isn't** sure. **He isn't** at home. **The store isn't** small. **It isn't** crowded.
We are not in the Laundromat. **They are not** on sale.	**We're not** in the Laundromat. **They're not** on sale.	**We aren't** in the Laundromat. **They aren't** on sale.

Language Note: There is only one negative short form for a plural noun + **are.**
   The cookies **aren't** free.

Compare affirmative and negative.

Affirmative	Negative
We **are** at the supermarket.	We **aren't** at home.
The cheese **is** fresh.	It **isn't** old.
I **am** new here.	I'm **not** sure about many things.
The samples **are** free.	The cookies **aren't** free.
You **are** from the U.S.	You're **not** confused.
Halina **is** a new immigrant.	Dorota **isn't** a new immigrant.

EXERCISE 1   Fill in the blanks with a negative form of the <u>underlined</u> verbs. Use short forms.

EXAMPLE   The supermarket <u>is</u> big. It ___*isn't*___ small.

1. The date <u>is</u> on packages. The date _____ on fruit.
2. We'<u>re</u> at the supermarket. We _____ at the Laundromat.
3. Bananas <u>are</u> 29¢ this week. They _____ 29¢ every week.
4. I'<u>m</u> in the supermarket. I _____ in the Laundromat.
5. The store <u>is</u> empty. It _____ crowded.
6. You'<u>re</u> helpful. You _____ confused.
7. Prices <u>are</u> on the shelves. They _____ on the products.
8. The sample cookies <u>are</u> free. The bags of cookies _____ free.

EXERCISE 2   Check the true statements. Change the other statements to the negative. Answers may vary.

EXAMPLE   _____✓_____ Supermarkets are big.

                 _____ I'm a new immigrant. *I'm not a new immigrant.*

1. _____ I'm confused about supermarkets.
2. _____ Life in the U.S. is easy.
3. _____ Supermarkets are clean.
4. _____ Americans are helpful.
5. _____ Supermarkets are crowded in the morning.
6. _____ Bags are free.
7. _____ Supermarkets are noisy.
8. _____ Prices are the same every week.

1.7 | Adjectives

An **adjective** gives a description of a noun.

Examples			Explanation
Subject	*Be*	Adjective	An adjective can follow the verb *be*.
The parking lot	is	**empty.**	subject + *be* + (*not*) + adjective
The store	isn't	**crowded.**	
The samples	are	**free.**	
Those are **free** samples.			An adjective can come before a noun.
These are **big** packages.			adjective + noun

Language Note: Descriptive adjectives are always singular. Only the noun is plural.
>   one **free** sample
>   two **free** samples

EXERCISE **3**   In each of the conversations below, fill in the blanks with an adjective from the box.

Vocabulary for Conversation A

new ✓	early	helpful	different
crowded	easy	big	

Conversation A: Halina and Dorota are at the supermarket.

Halina: I'm _____*new*_____ to this country. Everything is
               (example)
          _____ for me.
                  (1)

Dorota: Don't worry. I'm here with you.

Halina: You're very _____ .
                         (2)

Dorota: This is the supermarket. It's _____ to shop in a
                                          (3)
          supermarket.

Halina: This supermarket is _____. In my country, stores are
                                  (4)
          small.

Dorota: Bananas are on sale this week; only 29¢ a pound.

Halina: The supermarket and the parking lot aren't _____. Why
                                                          (5)
          not?

Dorota: It's only 10 a.m. It's _____.
                                     (6)

Vocabulary for Conversation B

small	open	different
hot	big	

Conversation B: Simon is showing a new immigrant, Victor, the Laundromat.

Simon: This is the Laundromat.

Victor: It's _____ in here.
(7)

Simon: Yes, it is. But the door is _____.
(8)

Victor: Some machines are _____ and some are _____.
(9) (10)

Simon: The big machines are for big items, like blankets.

Victor: All of these machines are the same, but those are _____.
(11)

Simon: These are washing machines. Those machines are dryers.

Victor: In my country, sometimes my wife is the washer and the air is the dryer!

1.8 | Expressions with *It*

Examples	Explanation
It's hot in the Laundromat. **It**'s cold outside.	Use *it* with weather or temperature.
It's 10 a.m. **It**'s early. **It** isn't late.	Use *it* with time.
It's easy **to wash** clothes at the Laundromat. **It** isn't hard. **It**'s early. **It**'s a good time **to shop**.	Use *it* with impersonal expressions: *it's easy, it's hard, it's good*. A *to*-phrase often follows.

EXERCISE 4   Fill in the blanks with one of the words from the list below. Answers may vary.

early	important	necessary	easy ✓
hard	good	hot	

EXAMPLE It's _____*easy*_____ to fill in the blanks.

1. It's _____ today.

2. It's _____. It's only 9:45. My class is at 10:00.

3. It isn't _____ to live in a new country.

4. It's _____ to learn English in the U.S.

5. It's _____ to learn a new language.

6. It isn't _____ to work and go to school.

1.9 | Singular and Plural

Singular	Plural	Rule
coin dime dollar	coin**s** dime**s** dollar**s**	Add -s to form the plural of most nouns.
dish watch	dish**es** watch**es**	Add -es to make the plural of nouns that end in -sh and -ch. Pronounce an extra syllable.
family baby	famil**ies** bab**ies**	Change final y to i and add -es when a word ends in a consonant + y.
day toy	day**s** toy**s**	Add only -s when a word ends in a vowel + y.
shelf life	shel**ves** li**ves**	Change final f or fe to –ves.

> **Pronunciation Note:** Sometimes we need to pronounce an extra syllable. Listen to your teacher pronounce these words.
> price—prices   noise—noises

EXERCISE 5   Fill in the blanks with the plural form of the noun in parentheses ( ).

EXAMPLE The _____*cars*_____ are in the parking lot.
                    (car)

1. The _____ are under the _____.
         (price)   (shelf)

2. The _____ are on the shelf.
         (match)

3. Some _____ are in the supermarket today.
           (baby)

4. It's Saturday and many _____ are at the supermarket.
                                    (family)

5. The soap for washing _____ costs $1.89.
                              (dish)

6. The _____ are on sale this week.
       (banana)

EDITING ADVICE

1. Use the correct form of *be*.

       are
   You ~~is~~ at the Laundromat.

2. Every sentence has a subject.

       It's
   ~~Is~~ 10:15 a.m.

       It's
   ~~Is~~ important to know English.

       It's
   ~~Is~~ hot in the Laundromat.

3. Don't confuse *this* and *these*.

       These
   ~~This~~ are big machines.

4. In a short form (contraction), put the apostrophe in place of the missing letter.

       You're
   ~~Your'e~~ late.

5. Use an apostrophe, not a comma, in a short form (contraction).

       I'm
   ~~I,m~~ at the supermarket.

6. Don't make adjectives plural.

   These are big~~s~~ machines.

EDITING QUIZ

Find the mistakes with the underlined words, and correct them. Not every sentence has a mistake. If the sentence is correct, write *C*.

                       are
EXAMPLES   We <u>is</u> late.

              The supermarket <u>is</u> big.   *C*

1. <u>Is</u> easy to use <u>this</u> dryers.

2. You <u>are'nt</u> late.

3. <u>She's not</u> in the bank.

4. <u>This</u> machines are empty.

5. We are <u>new</u> immigrants.

6. <u>Is</u> hot inside the Laundromat.

7. The machines are <u>hots</u>.

8. <u>I,m</u> late.

9. <u>Your'e</u> helpful.

1. What did you learn in this unit? Write three sentences in your notebook about each topic.
   - An American Laundromat
   - An American supermarket
   - Items in an American supermarket

2. Write three questions you still have about the Laundromat or supermarket.

EXPANSION ACTIVITIES

Writing Activity

Rewrite the following paragraph in your notebook. Change the singular nouns and pronouns to plurals. Change other necessary words, too.

This is a yellow apple. It's on sale. It's very big. It's only 75¢ a pound. That is a red apple. It isn't on sale. It's not very big. It's 75¢ a pound too. This is a free sample of the yellow apple. It's not very fresh. That's a free sample of the red apple. It is fresh. The red apple is good. The yellow apple isn't good today.

EXAMPLE *These are yellow apples.*

Outside Activities

1. Go to a supermarket in your neighborhood. Find an item on sale. Tell the class the usual price and the sale price. Find an item with samples. Tell the class the name of the item and the price.

2. Go to a Laundromat in your neighborhood. Tell the class the name and location. Find the price to wash and dry clothes.

Internet Activity

Search the words *online grocery store* or *online supermarket*. Find a common item. Find the price in two different online stores. Tell the class about the item and the prices.

UNIT

2

LESSON

GRAMMAR

Possessive Nouns
Possessive Adjectives

CONTEXT

My Clock Is Fast

 Circle *yes* or *no*.

1. I use a watch every day. YES   NO

2. I have a clock in every room of my house. YES   NO

MY CLOCK IS FAST

It's **Simon's** turn to help Victor today. But Simon is home. **His** wife, Marta, is at the hospital. **Marta's** father is sick. **Simon's** kids are home because today is a school holiday. So Dorota is here to help Victor at the bank.

Dorota: Hi, Victor. I'm here.

Victor: And Simon?

Dorota: He's busy. He's with **his** kids today. **Their** school is closed for a holiday. **His** wife is at the hospital with **her** father.

Victor: It's late. Look at **your** clock. It's 4:30. The bank is closed.

Dorota: No, it isn't. **My** clock is fast. It's only 4:15.

Victor: So **your** clock is broken.

Dorota: No, it isn't. **My** clock is always fast. And **my** watch is always fast. That way I'm always on time.

Victor: I'm confused. **Your** clock is fast, and that's OK with you?

Dorota: Yes. I'm never late. Time is important for Americans. **Their** ideas about time are different from **our** ideas about time

Dorota: We're here now. Oh, no. The bank is closed. Today is a holiday. It's Columbus Day. Come again tomorrow with Simon.

Vocabulary
in Context

turn	It's Simon's **turn** to help.
wife	Simon has a **wife**. Her name is Marta.
kid(s)	**Kids** are children.
holiday	It's a **holiday**. The school is closed.
clock	Look at the **clock**. It's 4:30.
fast	Your clock is **fast**.
on time	You're **on time**. You're not late.
broken	My clock isn't **broken**.
watch	My **watch** is fast. It's 4:15.

- On national holidays, the post office and most schools and banks are closed. Some businesses are open.
- Some American holidays are: New Year's Day, President's Day, Memorial Day, Independence Day, Labor Day, Thanksgiving, and Christmas.

Listening Activity

Listen to the sentences about the conversation. Circle *true* or *false*.

EXAMPLE (TRUE)   FALSE

1. TRUE   FALSE   4. TRUE   FALSE
2. TRUE   FALSE   5. TRUE   FALSE
3. TRUE   FALSE   6. TRUE   FALSE

2.1 | Possessive Nouns

Examples	Explanation
Simon's wife is at the hospital. **Marta's** father is sick. **Dorota's** clock isn't broken.	Use noun + 's to show ownership or relationship.

EXERCISE 1   Fill in the blanks with the correct form: *Marta's*, *Simon's*, or *Dorota's*.

EXAMPLE   ___Dorota's___ clock is fast.

1. _____ wife is Marta.

2. _____ father is sick.

3. Today it's _____ turn to help, but he's at home with the kids.

4. _____ language is Polish.

5. _____ language is Spanish.

EXERCISE 2   Fill in the blanks. Put the words in the correct order. Add an apostrophe (').

EXAMPLE   (kids/Simon) _____*Simon's kids*_____ aren't in school today.

1. (son/Victor) _____ isn't with him.

2. (children/Simon) _____ are at home.

3. (father/Marta) _____ is sick.

4. That's (car/Dorota) _____.

2.2 | Possessive Adjectives

Compare subject pronouns and possessive adjectives.

Examples	Explanation
I am late. **My** watch is slow.	I → **My**
You are late. **Your** watch is slow.	You → **Your**
He is late. **His** watch is slow.	He → **His**
She is late. **Her** watch is slow.	She → **Her**
We are late. **Our** clock is slow.	We → **Our**
They are late. **Their** clock is slow.	They → **Their**

EXERCISE **3**   Fill in the blanks with *my, your, his, her, our,* or *their*.

EXAMPLE   You are with ____*your*____ kids.

1. She is with _____ kids.
2. They are with _____ kids.
3. I am with _____ kids.

4. He is with _____ kids.
5. We are with _____ kids.

EXERCISE **4**   ABOUT YOU Circle *true* or *false*.

1. My watch is correct. TRUE   FALSE

2. Time is important to me. TRUE   FALSE

3. Money is important to me. TRUE   FALSE

4. I am with my classmates. Their language is different from my language. TRUE   FALSE

5. My teacher's name is hard for me. TRUE   FALSE

EXERCISE **5**   Simon and Dorota are on the telephone. Fill in the blanks with *my, your, his, her, their,* or *our*.

Simon: Hi, Dorota. This is Simon. I'm busy today. Marta's busy too.

_____ father is sick. _____ kids are at home today.
     (1)   (2)

_____ school is closed. It's _____ turn to help Victor
     (3)   (4)

today, but I'm busy.

Dorota: That's OK. _____ kids need you. I'm not busy today.
                              (5)

LESSON 2

GRAMMAR

Yes/No Questions and Short Answers
Singular and Plural—Irregular Forms

CONTEXT

Time Is Money

Before You Read Circle *yes* or *no*.

1. I'm usually on time. YES   NO

2. My doctor is usually on time. YES   NO

TIME IS MONEY

Simon: **Am I late?** I'm sorry. Traffic is bad today.
Victor: You're not late. It's only 10:15.
Simon: Oh, I'm 15 minutes late, then. I'm sorry.
Victor: Fifteen minutes is nothing.
Simon: In the U.S., people are usually on time.
Victor: Really? **Are you serious?**
Simon: Yes, I am.
Victor: **Are people on time for everything?**
Simon: For most things. They're on time for appointments.
Victor: **Is this an appointment?**
Simon: Yes, it is. I'm here to help you with the bank.
Victor: My doctor is never on time. She's always late.
Simon: That's different. Doctors are always behind schedule.
Victor: **Is it necessary to be on time with friends?**
Simon: It's not necessary, but it's polite.
Victor: Look. The time and temperature are outside the bank. **Is time always on your mind?**
Simon: Yes, it is. "Time is money." Time is always on our minds.

Vocabulary
in Context

traffic	I'm late. **Traffic** is bad today.
serious	Are you **serious?** Is it true?
appointment	She has an **appointment** with her doctor.
behind schedule	The doctor is **behind schedule.**
polite	It's **polite** to say "please" and "thank you."
temperature	The **temperature** is 75 degrees today.
on (my, your) mind	Time is always **on my mind.** I think about it a lot.
usually	Students are **usually** on time for class.
never	Some people are **never** on time.
always	Some people are **always** late.

Did You Know?

- Americans use Fahrenheit (F) for temperature. Other countries use Celsius (C).
- American banks often show time and temperature.

 **Listening Activity**   Listen to the following questions about the conversation. Circle the correct answer.

EXAMPLE   (Yes it is.)   No it isn't.

1. Yes, he is.   No, he isn't.
2. Yes, they are.   No, they aren't.
3. Yes, they are.   No, they aren't.
4. Yes, it is.   No, it isn't.
5. Yes, they are.   No, they aren't.

2.3 | *Yes/No* Questions and Short Answers

Put the form of *be* before the subject to ask a question.

Be	Subject	Complement	Short Answer
Am	I	late?	No, you aren't.
Is	traffic	bad?	Yes, it is.
Is	Simon	on time?	No, he isn't.
Are	you	serious?	Yes, I am.
Are	they	at the bank?	Yes, they are.

Compare statements and questions with *be*.

Statements	Questions
I am late.	**Am I** very late?
Time is important.	**Is time** always on your mind?
People are on time.	**Are people** always on time?
It is necessary to be on time.	**Is it** necessary to be on time with friends?

Pronunciation Note: A *yes/no* question has rising intonation. Listen to your teacher pronounce the statements and the questions above.

Punctuation Note: Put a question mark (?) at the end of a question.

EXERCISE 1   Fill in the form of *be* and a noun or pronoun to make a question.

EXAMPLES   ___*Are Simon and Victor*___ at the supermarket? No, they aren't.

                      ___*Are they*___ at the bank? Yes, they are.

1. _____ open? Yes, it is.

2. _____ late? No, you're not.

3. _____ necessary to be on time? No, it isn't.

4. _____ inside the bank? No, they aren't.

5. _____ on time? Yes, we are.

6. _____ polite? Yes, he is.

EXERCISE 2   Answer with a short answer.

EXAMPLE   Is the bank open? _____*Yes, it is*_____ .

1. Is Simon on time? _____ .

2. Are Simon and Victor at the bank? _____ .

3. Is Simon with Dorota? _____ .

4. Are doctors usually on time? _____ .

5. Is it necessary to be on time with friends? _____ .

6. Are Americans usually late for appointments? _____ .

EXERCISE 3   ABOUT YOU Answer with a short answer. You may work with a partner.

EXAMPLE   Are you usually on time?

Yes, I am.

1. Are you confused about some things in this country?

2. Is your apartment big?

3. Are you a serious student?

4. Are you an immigrant?

5. Are you an American citizen?

6. Is this class easy for you?

7. Is English hard for you?

8. Are your classmates from your native country?

9. Is this your first English class?

10. Is your dictionary new?

EXERCISE 4 Fill in the blanks.

Conversation A: Dorota and Victor

Bank of the South

Victor: _____ on time?
(1)

Dorota: Yes, you _____.
(2)

Victor: _____ at the bank?
(3)

Dorota: Yes, we _____. We're here to learn about the
(4)

bank.

Victor: _____ open?
(5)

Dorota: No, it _____. It's only 8:48. We're a few minutes
(6)

early.

Conversation B:
Simon and Marta

Simon: Hello?

Marta: Hi, Simon.

Simon: _____ in the car?
(7)

Marta: No, I'm _____. I'm at the supermarket now.
(8)

Simon: It's 9 p.m. _____ open now?
(9)

Marta: Yes, it _____. This store is open 24 hours a day.
(10)

Simon: _____ serious?
(11)

Marta: Yes, I am.

Simon: We need bananas. _____ on sale?
(12)

Marta: Yes, they _____. They're only 29¢ a pound this
(13)

week.

Simon: Buy bread too. _____ fresh?
(14)

Marta: Yes, it is. It's still warm.

2.4 | Singular and Plural—Irregular Forms

Singular	Plural	Explanation
child person	children people	Sometimes the plural form is a different word.
man woman	men women	Sometimes the plural form has a vowel change.
Pronunciation Note: You hear the difference between *woman* and *women* in the first syllable. Listen to your teacher pronounce the singular and plural forms.		

EXERCISE 5 Fill in the blanks with the plural form of the noun in parentheses ( ).

EXAMPLE The _____*men*_____ are late.
(man)

1. Two _____ are in front of the bank.
(person)

2. _____ are in the supermarket.
(child)

3. Two _____ are in front of me.
(woman)

4. The _____ are in line.
(man)

EXERCISE 6 Fill in the blanks with *is* or *are*.

EXAMPLE The people _____*are*_____ helpful.

1. The child _____ with her mother.
2. The woman _____ busy.
3. A person _____ alone.
4. The people _____ on time.
5. The children _____ with their parents.
6. The man _____ late.

LESSON 3

GRAMMAR

Information Questions
Articles *A/An*

CONTEXT

At the ATM

Before You Read

Circle *yes* or *no*.

1. I have a bank account. YES   NO
2. I have an ATM card. YES   NO

AT THE ATM

Dorota: Hi, Victor. **How are you?**

Victor: Fine, thanks. **Where are we?**

Dorota: We're at the First Community Bank.

Victor: **What time is it?**

Dorota: It's 7:30 p.m. The bank is closed now.

Victor: **When is the bank open?**

Dorota: This bank is open from 9 to 4, Monday through Thursday. It's open from 9 to 7 on Friday and 9 to 1 on Saturday.

Victor: **Who's that woman inside?**

Dorota: She's a security guard.

Victor: **Why are we here?**

Dorota: I need cash. I need to go to the supermarket. The ATM is always open.

Victor: **What's an ATM?**

Dorota: ATM means Automatic Teller Machine. It's a machine for cash.

Victor: **What's that?**

Dorota: This is my bank card. It's the key to open the door and get cash.

Victor: Is it easy to get cash?

Dorota: Yes, it is. But a PIN is necessary. And cash in your account, of course!

Victor: **What's a PIN?**

Dorota It's a personal identification number.

Victor: **What's your PIN?**

Dorota: That's a secret!

Vocabulary in Context

security guard	The **security guard** is in the bank.
ATM	The **ATM** is always open.
cash	We are at the bank. We need **cash.**
PIN	A **PIN** is a personal identification number.
account	I have a bank **account.**
secret	No one knows the number. It's a **secret.**
of course	A: Is the ATM always open? B: Yes, **of course.**
through	The bank is open Monday **through** Friday.

You can do your banking online too.
- Pay bills
- Transfer money
- Invest

 **Listening Activity**   Listen to the following questions about the conversation. Circle the answer.

EXAMPLE   (At the bank.)   At the supermarket.

1.	Yes, it's late.	It's 10:15.
2.	24 hours a day	Monday through Saturday
3.	from 9 to 4	24 hours a day
4.	It's a machine for cash.	It's at the bank.
5.	at 10:15	To get cash.
6.	924	It's a secret.

2.5 | Information Questions

Information questions begin with *where, when, why, who, what,* and *how*. Observe the word order in an information question.

Question Word	Be	Subject + . . .	Answer
Where	are	we?	We're at the ATM.
What	is	that?	It's a machine.
What time	is	it?	It's 10:15.
Why	are	we here?	We're here to get cash.
When	is	the bank open?	It's open from Monday through Saturday.
Who	is	that woman?	She's a security guard.
How	are	you?	I'm fine, thanks.

Language Notes:
1. Study the meaning of the information question words:

    where = place   *why* = reason   *when* = time   *how* = health

    what = thing   *who* = person   *what time* = exact time   *how old* = age

2. You can make a short form (contraction) with information words and *is*.

    What's that?   **When's** the bank open?

    Who's she?   **Why's** he here?

Compare statements and information questions.	
Statements	**Questions**
The bank is open.	When **is the bank** open?
We are at the ATM.	Why **are we** at the ATM?
You are a student.	How old **are you?**
I am at a bank.	Where **am I?**
She is inside the bank.	Why **is she** inside the bank?
Dorota is from Poland.	Who **is Dorota?**

Pronunciation Note: Information questions have a falling intonation. Listen to your teacher pronounce the statements on the left and the questions on the right.

EXERCISE 1 Write a question word.

Dorota: _____*How*_____ are you?
        (example)

Victor: I'm fine. _____ are we?
              (1)

Dorota: We're at the Laundromat.

Victor: _____'s that?
        (2)

Dorota: It's a dryer.

Victor: _____ are we here?
        (3)

Dorota: To learn about the Laundromat.

Victor: _____'s that woman?
        (4)

Dorota: She's the manager.

Victor: _____ is the Laundromat open?
        (5)

Dorota: Every day from 7 a.m. to 9 p.m.

Victor: _____ is it?
        (6)

Dorota: 8:45. We're late!

EXERCISE **2** Complete the question.

EXAMPLE It's late. What time ___*is it*___ ?

1. They're at the bank. Why _____ ?
2. I'm fine. How _____ ?
3. The bank is open today. What time _____ ?
4. We're late. Why _____ ?
5. The ATM is nere here. Where _____ ?
6. That woman is in the bank. Who _____ ?

EXERCISE **3** ABOUT YOU Answer the questions. Write a sentence.

1. Where are you from? _____
2. What's your name? _____
3. Who's your English teacher? _____
4. Where's your English teacher from? _____
5. Where's your school? _____
6. When is the school open? _____
7. When are you at home? _____
8. Why are you here? _____

2.6 | Articles *A/An*

Use *a/an* before a singular noun to identify the subject.

Examples	Explanation
What's this? It's **a** bank. Who's that woman? She's **a** security guard.	Use *a* before a consonant sound.
What's that? It's **an** ATM. I'm **an** immigrant.	Use *an* before a vowel sound. The vowels are *a, e, i, o,* and *u.*

What are those? They're ATMs.
Quarters and dimes are coins.
	Do not use *a/an* before a plural noun.
	    Wrong: They're *an* ATMs.
	    Wrong: Quarters and dimes are *a* coins.

The bank is big. It's **a** big bank.	Use *a* or *an* before an adjective only if a noun follows the adjective. *Wrong:* The bank is *a* big.

EXERCISE 4 Fill in the blanks with *a* or *an*.

This is _____*a*_____ bank.

That's _____*an*_____ ATM.

1. I'm _____ immigrant.

2. I'm _____ new immigrant.

3. This is _____ PIN.

4. This is _____ easy PIN.

5. A quarter is _____ coin.

6. Simon isn't _____ old man.

7. Dorota is from Poland. Poland is _____ eastern European country.

8. I'm _____ busy person.

EXERCISE 5 Fill in the blanks with the correct form of *be* and *a* or *an*. Do not use *a* or *an* with plural nouns.

Victor: What's that?

Dorota: It _'s an_ ATM.
                  (example)

Victor: What's an ATM?

Dorota: It _____ machine for cash.
                  (1)

Victor: What are these?

Dorota: These _____ envelopes.
                    (2)

Victor: What are they for?

Dorota: Depositing checks.

Victor: What _____ check?
                   (3)

Dorota: Look. This _____ check. It _____ paycheck.
                        (4)   *(5)*

Victor: What _____ those?
                   (6)

Dorota: Those _____ drive-up ATMs.
                    (7)

Victor: Americans _____ busy people. They _____ always
                         (8)   *(9)*

in their cars.

Dorota: It _____ easy way to use the bank.
                  (10)

EXERCISE 6 Add the adjective in parentheses ( ) to the sentence. Change *a* to *an* or *an* to *a* if needed.

EXAMPLE It's a bank. (old).
It's an old bank.

1. You are an immigrant. (new)

   _____

2. You're a person. (busy)

   _____

3. I'm an American. (new)

   _____

4. This is a way to get cash. (easy)

   _____

5. That's a machine. (empty)

   _____

6. He's a man. (helpful)

   _____

1. *People* is a plural word. Use a plural verb.

   The new people ~~is~~ late. *(are)*

2. Use the correct possessive adjective.

   She is with ~~his~~ father. *(her)*   They are with ~~they~~ mother. *(their)*

3. Don't confuse *you're* and *your.*

   What's ~~you're~~ name? *(your)*   ~~Your~~ never late. *(You're)*

4. Use the correct word order in a question.

   Why ~~you are~~ late? *(are you)*   Is ~~big the supermarket~~? *(the supermarket big)*

5. Use *a* or *an* before a singular noun.

   E is ⌃ vowel. This is ⌃ easy lesson. *(a)* *(an)*

6. Don't use *a* or *an* with plural nouns.
   Victor and Dorota are ~~an~~ immigrants.

EDITING QUIZ

Find the mistakes with the underlined words, and correct them. Not every sentence has a mistake. If the sentence is correct, write *C.*

EXAMPLES   You are ⌃ nice person. *(a)*
    Simon and Dorota are nice people.   *C*

1. Why we are here?
2. Is it 10:15 now?
3. When the bank is open?
4. Where is the bank?
5. She's a kind woman.
6. Dorota is at the hospital. His father is sick.
7. He is a old man.
8. Where's you're book?
9. Ten people is in the bank.
10. Who are those people? What are they names?
11. *U* is vowel.
12. *A E I O U* are a vowels.

1. What did you learn in this unit? Write three sentences in your notebook about each topic.
   - Time in the United States
   - ATM machines

2. Write three questions you still have about ATM machines or time in the U.S.

EXPANSION ACTIVITIES

Writing Activities

1. In your notebook, write a short paragraph of five to six sentences about Marta and her daughter, Amy, in the picture.

   EXAMPLE *Marta is with her daughter, Amy.*

2. In your notebook, rewrite the following paragraph. Change *I* to *Simon and Marta*. Make all the necessary changes in verbs and possessive pronouns.

I'm at the bank early today. It's a bank near my work place. It's not open. But I'm not worried. The ATM machine is always open. This bank is not my bank. It's $1.50 to get my cash here. But it's easy to get cash with my ATM card.

   EXAMPLE *Simon and Marta are at the bank early today.*

Outside Activity

Find a bank in your neighborhood. Tell the class the name and address of the bank. When is the bank open? Where is the ATM machine?

Internet Activity

Search the words *exact time* or *official clock*. Find the time in your part of the country. Then look at your watch. What time is it on your watch?

UNIT

3

GRAMMAR

Imperatives
Let's
Object Pronouns

CONTEXT

Filling Out Forms

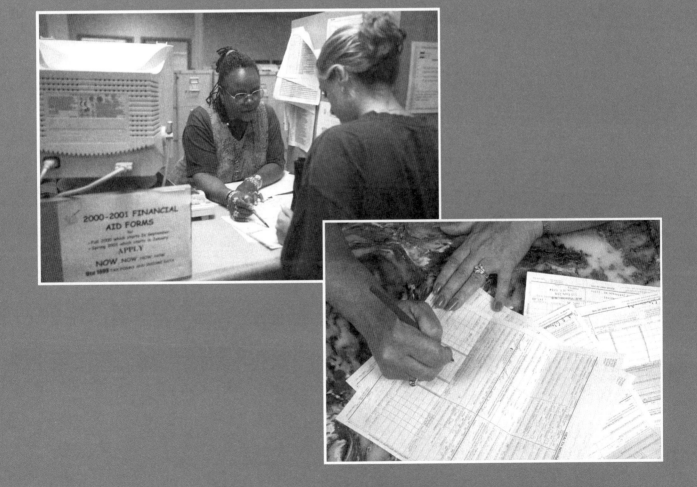

GRAMMAR

Imperative Forms—Affirmative
Imperative Forms—Negative

CONTEXT

Getting a Social Security Card

Before You Read

Circle *yes* or *no*.

1. I have a Social Security card. YES   NO

2. I write the day before the month (November 6 = 11/6). YES   NO

GETTING A SOCIAL SECURITY CARD

This is a conversation between Dorota and Halina.

Dorota: I have something for you. **Look.**
Halina: What is it?
Dorota: It's an application. It's for a Social Security card.
Halina: I'm not sure what to do.
Dorota: **Don't worry.** It's easy. **Let** me help.
Halina: OK. I have a pencil.
Dorota: No, no. **Don't use** a pencil. **Use** a blue or black pen.
Halina: OK.
Dorota: Here's a pen. **Fill** out all the information. **Print,** but **sign** in Box 16.

Halina: I'm finished.
Dorota: What's your date of birth?
Halina: 11-6-70.
Dorota: Is your birthday in November?
Halina: No. It's in June.
Dorota: **Don't write** 11-6. **Write** the month, then the day. That's the American way.
Halina: OK. 6-11-70.
Dorota: **Don't write** 70. **Write** 1970.

Halina: I'm finished. What's next?
Dorota: **Don't forget. Sign** your name. **Make** a copy of your birth certificate. Then **go** to the Social Security office. **Take** your birth certificate and another identity document with you.

Vocabulary in Context

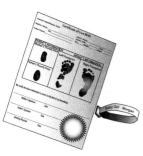

application	This is an **application** for a Social Security card.
let	**Let** me help you.
fill out	**Fill out** the application with a pen.
print	**Print** the information. Don't write it. *Halina Laski*
sign	**Sign** your name. *Halina Laski*
date of birth	My **date of birth** is June 11.
birthday	My **birthday** is June 11.
forget	Don't **forget** your Social Security number.
birth certificate	A new baby has a **birth certificate.**
identity document	Here's my driver's license. It's my **identity document.** It shows who I am.

- On an application, DOB means *date of birth*.
- Identity documents include:

Driver's license   Marriage certificate

Passport   School ID (identification) card

Listening Activity

Listen to these instructions. If the instruction is correct for the Social Security application, circle *true*. If the instruction is not correct, circle *false*.

EXAMPLE (TRUE)   FALSE

1. TRUE FALSE	4. TRUE FALSE
2. TRUE FALSE	5. TRUE FALSE
3. TRUE FALSE	6. TRUE FALSE

3.1 | Imperative Forms—Affirmative

Use the imperative:
- to give instructions or directions
- to give suggestions
- to get someone's attention

Examples	Explanation
Look at this. **Use** a pen. **Write** your date of birth.	Use the base form of the verb for the imperative.
Help me, **please.** **Please** help me.	Add *please* to be more polite.

EXERCISE 1 Fill in the blanks with one of the verbs from the box below.

Fill	Use	Take	Sign
Go	Write	Make ✓	Help

EXAMPLE ___Make___ a copy of your birth certificate.

1. I'm confused. _____ me, please.

2. _____ out the application today.

3. _____ a pen.

4. _____ the month before the day.

5. _____ to the Social Security office today.

6. _____ your birth certificate with you.

7. _____ your name in Box 16.

3.2 | Imperative Forms—Negative

Examples	Explanation
Don't worry. **Don't write** 11-6 for June 11. **Don't forget.**	Use *do not* + base form for the negative. The short form (contraction) is *don't*.

EXERCISE 2 Fill in the blanks with the negative imperative of a verb from the box below.

put	print	be	forget
worry ✓	write	drive	

EXAMPLE It's not hard. ___Don't worry___. I can help you.

1. Take your papers with you. _____.

2. Stay here. _____ your car to the Social Security office now.

3. Print. _____ your information.

4. Be on time. _____ late.

5. Stop. _____ one more word on the application.

6. Sign your name in Box 16. _____ it.

EXERCISE 3 Fill in the blanks with an affirmative or negative imperative. Use the verbs from the box below.

use	put	worry ✓
forget	write	bring

EXAMPLE _____*Don't worry*_____ about the application. I am here to help.

1. _____ a pencil to fill out your application.

2. _____ to sign your application at the end.

3. _____ two forms of ID with you to the Social Security office.

4. _____ all four numbers for the year (*1970*, not *70*).

5. _____ the day first in your date of birth.

EXERCISE 4 This is a conversation between Amy and her mother, Marta. Fill in the blanks with one of the verbs from the box below. Use two verbs twice.

don't ask	make ✓	wash	say
don't touch	let	be	give

Amy: _____Make_____ me a jelly sandwich, Mommy.
       (example)

Marta: I'm busy now. Later.

Amy: What's that, Mommy?

Marta: It's my application. Your hands are dirty. _____
                                                              (1)
the application.

Amy: What's an application, Mommy? And what's that?

Marta: It's my birth certificate. Please _____ so many
                                               (2)
questions. Mommy's busy now.

Amy: I'm thirsty. _____ me a glass of milk, Mommy.
                         (3)

Marta: Later. _____ quiet now, please, and
                     (4)

_____ me finish. This is very important.
    (5)

Marta: OK. I'm finished now.

Amy: _____ me a jelly sandwich.
            (6)

Marta: _____, "Please."
              (7)

Amy: Please.

Marta: And _____ your hands.
                  (8)

Marta: Here is your sandwich and milk. _____ "Thank you."
                                              (9)

Amy: Thank you, Mommy.

Lesson 1   49

LESSON 2

GRAMMAR

Let's
Compare Subject and Object Pronouns

CONTEXT

Financial Aid Application

Before You Read

Circle *yes* or *no*.

1. I have financial aid.
   YES   NO

2. Online forms
   are easy.
   YES   NO

DISTRICT FINANCIAL AID APPLICATION

SECTION 1: To be completed by the STUDENT   STUDENT'S DISTRICT ☐

After Completing Section 1 - please mail to the Financial Aid Office of the Concordia of your choice!

NOTE TO STUDENT: Your District may require additional financial and/or other information. Please comply
                   promply with their request in order to expedite your application.

Last Name:	First Name	MI	
			Soc. Sec. No.
Date of Birth:	Preferred Mailing Address		
	Street Address:		
Telephone:			E-Mail address:
	City:	State:	Zip:	

While in school you intend to live:	Marital Status:	Total number of your dependents: _____
___ with parents ___ on-campus ___ off-campus	S __ M __ D __	Self (___) Spouse (___) Children (___)

Do you intend to enter full-time church work? ___Yes ___ No	Your Home Congregation/City:	Your Pastor's Signature

Major Course of Study:

FINANCIAL AID APPLICATION

Halina and Shafia are friends from English class.

Halina: College is expensive in the U.S.

Shafia: Yes, it is.

Halina: **Let's go** to the financial aid office at the college tomorrow. **Let's get** an application.

Shafia: That's not necessary. **Let's go** on the Internet and get an application.

Halina: Are the applications online?

Shafia: Yes, they are.

Halina: You're right. Here's the financial aid Web site. The application is here.

Shafia: **Let's fill** out the application online. It's easy. Enter your Social Security number.

Halina: That's an easy question.

Shafia: Don't use dashes.

Halina: OK. 354003421.

Shafia: Now enter your first and last names. Next, create a password.

Halina: OK. Don't look at my password. What about this question? What's a middle initial?

Shafia: I don't know. **Let's call** Dorota.

Halina: It's after 10 p.m. **Let's not call** now. **Let's not** bother her. **Let's look up** the words in the dictionary.

Shafia: Good idea.

354-00-3421
↑ ↑
dashes

Vocabulary in Context

expensive	College is **expensive** in the U.S.
financial aid	**Financial aid** is money to help pay for college.
available	Financial aid is **available** for some students.
online	The application is available **online.** It's on the Internet.
dash(es)	Write your Social Security number. Don't use **dashes.**
create a password	**Create a password.** It's a secret number or word.
enter	**Enter** your name on line 3 on the computer application.
what about	**What about** this question? What is it?
middle initial	My name is Dorota R. Nowak. My **middle initial** is R.
bother	Let's not **bother** her. She's busy.
look up	**Look up** the word in the dictionary.

Did You Know?

Many Americans have a middle name.
- Nicole *Anne* Jackson
- Brian *Robert* Goldberg

Listening Activity

Listen to the sentences about the conversation. Circle *true* or *false*.

EXAMPLE TRUE (FALSE)

1. TRUE FALSE
2. TRUE FALSE
3. TRUE FALSE

4. TRUE FALSE
5. TRUE FALSE
6. TRUE FALSE

3.3 | Let's

Examples	Explanation
Let's go to the office. **Let's get** an application.	Use *let's* + base form to make a suggestion. *Let's* is a contraction for *let us*.
Let's not call now.	Use *let's not* + base form to make the negative.

EXERCISE 1 Fill in the blanks with *let's* or *let's not* and one of the verbs from the box below. Use two of the verbs twice.

walk	fill it out	go ✓
get	call	drive

EXAMPLE ___*Let's go*___ to the financial aid office.

1. _____ to the financial aid office. It's not far.

2. _____. It's very cold today. Let's _____.

3. It's not necessary to go to the office. _____ an application online.

4. This application is easy. _____ now.

5. I don't understand "middle initial." Where's the telephone?
   _____ Dorota now.

6. It's late. _____ now. Let's call tomorrow.

3.4 | Compare Subject and Object Pronouns

Examples	Explanation
I am confused. Help **me**. **You** are not alone. I am here to help **you**. **He** is at home. Don't bother **him**. **She** is at home. Don't bother **her**. **It** is your date of birth. Write **it**. **We** are busy. Don't bother **us**. **They** are confused. Help **them**.	Put the subject pronoun before the verb. Put the object pronoun after the verb. Compare subject pronouns and object pronouns. <table><tr><th>Subject Pronoun</th><th>Object Pronoun</th></tr><tr><td>I</td><td>me</td></tr><tr><td>you</td><td>you</td></tr><tr><td>he</td><td>him</td></tr><tr><td>she</td><td>her</td></tr><tr><td>it</td><td>it</td></tr><tr><td>we</td><td>us</td></tr><tr><td>they</td><td>them</td></tr></table>
I am finished *with* **it**. This application is *for* **you**. This question is *about* **me**.	Use the object pronoun after a preposition: *with, for, about, to, on, in, of, at,* or *from*.

EXERCISE **2** Fill in the blanks with an object pronoun.

EXAMPLE I'm confused. Please help ___*me*___.

1. Dorota is helpful. Let's call _____.

2. I'm busy. Don't bother _____.

3. We are confused. Please help _____.

4. Simon is busy. Don't bother _____.

5. I'm busy. Ask your father. Ask _____ for help.

6. Dorota and Simon are helpful. Let's ask _____.

7. The application is necessary. Let's fill _____ out.

8. This is my password. Don't look at _____.

9. Are you confused? Don't worry. I'm here to help _____.

10. Mother knows the answer. Let's ask _____.

EXERCISE 3 Fill in the blanks with the object or subject pronoun.

EXAMPLE We are with them. _____They_____ are with _____us_____.

1. I am with you. _____ are with _____.
2. She is with him. _____ is with _____.
3. They are with us. _____ are with _____.
4. You are with me. _____ am with _____.
5. She is with them. _____ are with _____.

EXERCISE 4 Fill in the blanks with the object or subject pronoun.

Shafia: What's that?

Halina: _____It_____'s an application for financial aid. College is
(example)

expensive in the U.S. We're immigrants. It's very expensive

for _____.
_(1)_

Shafia: It's expensive for Americans too. But it's easy for

_____ to fill out the application. It isn't easy for
_(2)_

_____. I don't understand one question. I'm confused
_(3)_

about _____.
_(4)_

Shafia: Let's call Dorota.

Halina: _____'s late. It's after 10 p.m. Maybe _____'s
_(5)_   _(6)_

asleep. Let's call _____ tomorrow.
_(7)_

Shafia: Or call Simon.

Halina: _____'s busy. His wife's father is sick. She's with
_(8)_

_____ in the hospital. Simon's with his kids. He's with
_(9)_

_____ all day.
_(10)_

Shafia: Let's read the application together. Maybe _____ can
_(11)_

do _____ together.
_(12)_

Halina: Let's try.

EDITING ADVICE

1. Use *don't* to make a negative imperative.

   Don't
   ~~Not~~ write here.

2. Use *not* after *let's* to make the negative.

        not
   Let's ~~don't~~ be late.

3. Don't use *to* after *don't*.

   Don't ~~to~~ write on this line.

4. Don't use *to* after *let's*.

   Let's ~~to~~ eat now.

5. Don't forget the apostrophe in *let's*.

   Let's
   ~~Lets~~ go home.

6. Use the subject pronoun before the verb.

   They
   ~~Them~~ are good students.

7. Use the object pronoun after the verb or preposition.

        him   them
   Don't bother ~~he~~.   Look at ~~they~~.

EDITING QUIZ

Find the mistakes with the underlined words, and correct them. Not every sentence has a mistake. If the sentence is correct, write *C*.

EXAMPLES   Your mother is busy. Please help <u>she</u>. *(her)*

               It's late. <u>Let's go</u> now.   *C*

1. <u>They</u> are busy now. Don't bother <u>they</u>.

2. <u>She</u> is confused. Please help <u>she</u>.

3. <u>Don't to</u> bother Simon. <u>Him</u> is busy.

4. <u>Let's</u> read the book together.

5. <u>Let's not</u> speak Spanish in class. <u>Lets</u> speak English now.

6. <u>Don't</u> talk about <u>me</u>.

7. This is my PIN. <u>Don't to look</u> at <u>it</u>.

8. Let's walk. <u>Let's don't drive</u>.

1. What did you learn in this unit? Write three imperative sentences in your notebook about each of these topics:
   - How to fill out a Social Security card application
   - How to fill out a financial aid application

2. Write three questions you still have about Social Security cards or financial aid for students.

EXPANSION ACTIVITIES

Writing Activities

1. Rewrite these instructions in your notebook. Put the sentences in the correct order.

   How to Get a Social Security Card

   Photocopy your birth certificate.
   Take or send all your documents to the Social Security office.
   Get an application from a Social Security office or online.
   Find another identity document.
   Don't forget to sign the form.
   Fill out all the necessary information.
   Don't write the information. Print it.

2. Rewrite the following paragraph in your notebook. Change all the underlined nouns to object pronouns.

   This is a financial aid application. Read the financial aid application carefully. Write your name and Social Security number on the financial aid application. Dashes are always in a Social Security number. Don't write the dashes on the application. Some questions are difficult. Ask about difficult questions. Dorota is helpful. Ask Dorota for help. The man at the financial aid office is helpful too. Ask the man for help.

   EXAMPLE   *This is a financial aid application. Read it carefully.*

Outside Activity

Find the financial aid office at your school. Ask for a financial aid application. Practice filling it out.

Internet Activity

Go to the Social Security Web site (**www.ssa.gov**) and click on *Use Your Zip to Find our Office*. Find the address of a Social Security office near you.

UNIT

4

GRAMMAR
The Simple Present Tense
Frequency Words

CONTEXT
American Lifestyles

GRAMMAR

The Simple Present Tense—Affirmative Statements
Spelling of the **-s** Form
Uses of the Simple Present Tense
Frequency Words

CONTEXT

Having Fun

Before You Read

1. What are your free-time activities?

2. What is your favorite summer activity?

Americans **work** hard. But they **have** fun too. Americans **do** many different activities in their free time. They often **visit** with family and friends. But a visitor usually **needs** an invitation. Or the visitor **calls** first.

People sometimes **invite** their friends to their homes. Sometimes, they **watch** sports on TV. One popular game is the Super Bowl. The two best football teams in the U.S. **play** in January or February every year. Friends often **watch** this game together.

Americans **like** the movies. They often **go** to the movies on weekends. But theaters are open every day. Theaters **sell** popcorn, candy, and soft drinks. People **eat** at the movies.

People with children often **spend** time at school activities. City parks **have** many fun activities too. Americans also **enjoy** museums. Museums **have** many learning activities. A list of activities is usually on your city's Web site.

In warm weather, Americans often **go** to outdoor concerts. Many city parks **have** free concerts in the summer. People sometimes **eat** outside too. They **have** picnics. They **cook** on a grill. We **call** this kind of food "barbeque." It is very popular.

Vocabulary in Context	
have fun	I **have fun** at the museum. I am happy there.
activity(ies)	City parks often have free **activities,** or fun things to do.
team	One baseball **team** has many players.
outdoor concert(s)	She likes **outdoor concerts.** She listens to music outside.
grill	I like to cook outside. I use my **grill** for cooking.
enjoy	They **enjoy** the Super Bowl. They are happy to watch this game.
spend time	She **spends** a lot of **time** with her daughter. She is with her daughter often.
invite/ invitation	Americans **invite** their friends to their homes. They ask their friends to visit them. This is an **invitation.**
each other	They like **each other.** He likes her and she likes him.
best	We are a good team, but they are the **best** team.

Listening Activity

Listen to the sentences about the reading. Circle *true* or *false*.

EXAMPLE (TRUE)   FALSE

1. TRUE FALSE		5. TRUE FALSE
2. TRUE FALSE		6. TRUE FALSE
3. TRUE FALSE		7. TRUE FALSE
4. TRUE FALSE		

4.1 | The Simple Present Tense—Affirmative Statements

A simple present tense verb has two forms: the base form and the *-s* form.

Subject	Verb (Base Form)	Complement
I	**like**	concerts.
You	**have**	a grill.
We	**go**	to the movies.
They	**buy**	popcorn at the movies.
Americans	**enjoy**	museums.

Subject	Verb (-s Form)	Complement
He	**likes**	popcorn.
She	**has**	a lot of friends.
Simon	**enjoys**	the Super Bowl.
My family	**spends**	a lot of time in the park.
Our team	**plays**	every Saturday.

Language Notes:

1. Three verbs have an irregular *-s* form: *go (he goes)*, *do (she does)*, and *have (it has)*.
2. *Family* and *team* are singular nouns.

EXERCISE 1 Fill in the blanks with the correct form of the affirmative simple present tense. Use the verb in parentheses ( ).

EXAMPLE He ___*goes*___ to the movies on the weekends.
(go)

1. Kids _____ activities in parks.
(like)

2. That family _____ many things together.
(do)

3. We _____ a lot of time with our friends.
(spend)

4. My park usually _____ summer activities.
(have)

5. Americans _____ before a visit to a friend's house.
(call)

6. My daughter often _____ her friends to our home.
(invite)

4.2 | Spelling of the *-s* Form

Examples	Explanation
visit—visit**s** like—like**s**	Add **-s** to most verbs to make the -s form.
kiss—kiss**es** wash—wash**es** watch—watch**es** fix—fix**es**	Add **-es** to base forms with *ss, sh, ch,* or *x* at the end.
worry—worr**ies** try—tr**ies**	If the base form ends in a consonant + *y*, change *y* to **-i** and add **-es.**
pay—pa**ys** play—pla**ys**	If the base form ends in a vowel + *y,* do not change the **y**. Just add **-s.**

EXERCISE 2 Fill in the blanks with the -s form of the verb in parentheses ( ).

EXAMPLE The team ___*plays*___ baseball.
(play)

1. Each football team _____ to win the Super Bowl.
(try)

2. Simon's son _____ TV every night.
(watch)

3. Dorota _____ football games.
(enjoy)

4. A new immigrant sometimes _____ about life here.
   (worry)

5. Only one team _____ the Super Bowl.
   (win)

6. Her father _____ the grill after a barbeque.
   (wash)

7. He _____ a lot of time outside in summer.
   (spend)

4.3 | Uses of the Simple Present Tense

Examples	Explanation
American movie theaters **sell** popcorn.	Use the simple present tense for facts.
We **go** to the movies once a week.	Use the simple present for repeated actions, such as customs and habits.
Americans **like** the movies.	Use the simple present with *like, need*, and *want*.

EXERCISE 3 Write a sentence with the correct form of the verb in the simple present tense. Use the ideas in the reading.

EXAMPLE Americans / like
Americans like outdoor concerts.

1. American museums / have

   _____

2. An American visitor / need

   _____

3. Two teams / play

   _____

4. People / invite

   _____

5. An American family / go

   _____

6. Americans / cook

   _____

7. The best football team / win

   _____

4.4 | Frequency Words

Frequency	Frequency Word	Examples
100% ↕ 0%	always	Americans **always** call before a visit.
	usually	People **usually** enjoy their free time.
	often	She **often** goes to the movies.
	sometimes	Women **sometimes** watch sports with their husbands.
	rarely	Americans **rarely** visit friends without an invitation.
	hardly ever	Some Americans **hardly ever** have free time.
	never	I **never** cook outside in January.

Language Note: Frequency words go before the verb. *Often, usually,* and *sometimes* can also go at the beginning or at the end of the sentence.

Sometimes we go to the movies.

We go to the movies **often.**

Usually she eats breakfast.

EXERCISE **4** ABOUT YOU Write a sentence with the words given. Add a frequency word from the chart above.

EXAMPLE speak English at home
I hardly ever speak English at home.

1. cook dinner at home

   _____

2. watch TV in the evening

   _____

3. invite my friends to my home

   _____

4. visit my friends without an invitation

   _____

5. spend time at museums

   _____

6. work on Saturdays

   _____

EXERCISE 5 Complete the sentences in Dorota's talk about American customs. Use the words given in the correct order.

_____Americans often invite_____ each other to dinner.
(example: Americans/invite/often)

_____ a guest for a specific day and time.
(1. an American/invite/usually)

"Let's have dinner sometime" is not an invitation.

_____ on time. It isn't polite to be more than
(2. a dinner guest/come/always)

15 minutes late. _____ something for the host
(3. guests/bring/usually)

or hostess. _____ flowers.
(4. they/bring/sometimes)

_____ candy. At dinner,
(5. they/bring/sometimes)

_____ something nice about the food or the
(6. guests/say/often)

table. It is polite in the U.S. _____ for more
(7. guests/ask/sometimes)

food. It is common in the U.S.

EXERCISE 6 Fill in the blanks in Simon's phone conversation with Victor. Use the verbs in the box below. Use two verbs twice.

pays	have	sells	likes
plays	has ✓	need	enjoy

Simon: Are you and Lisa busy tonight?

Victor: No, why?

Simon: The city _____has_____ concerts in the park on Thursday
                    (example)
evenings. Let's all go tonight.

Victor: Sure. It's a great idea.

Simon: Bring Maya. Kids _____ outdoor concerts.
                              (1)

Victor: How much are the tickets?

Simon: The city _____ for these concerts. They're free for all
of us.   (2)

Victor: Where is it?

Simon: It's at Logan Park on Central Street. A different band

_____ there every Thursday evening from 7 to 9. The
        (3)

kids _____ fun with their friends. A little store in the
            (4)

park _____ popcorn and ice cream. My daughter,
            (5)

Amy, _____ ice cream in the summer. Marta and I
            (6)

_____ the different kinds of music.
        (7)

Victor: We _____ chairs, right?
                    (8)

Simon: Yes, but I _____ some extra chairs for outside.
                              (9)

They're easy to carry. Don't worry about that. Just be at our
house about 6:30.

Victor: Thanks, Simon. See you tonight!

LESSON 2

GRAMMAR

Simple Present Tense—Negative Forms
Expressions of Time with the Simple Present Tense
Infinitives with Simple Present Verbs

CONTEXT

Working in the U.S.

Before You Read

1. What is your job?
2. Do you like your job? Why or why not?

WORKING IN THE U.S.

Work is very important to Americans. They often ask each other about their jobs. But they **don't ask** each other about their salaries or wages.

Americans usually work five days a week. Most office workers and teachers **don't work** on Saturdays and Sundays. But many people have other days off. Workers in stores and restaurants hardly ever have days off on weekends. Stores and restaurants are very busy on weekends.

A day's work is usually eight hours, or 40 hours a week. But most Americans work more. Some people complain. They **don't like** to work so many hours. But others want to make more money. People with wages **get** more money for each hour of overtime work.

Many people **don't relax** on their days off. A day off **doesn't** always **mean** free time. Some people get part-time jobs on these days.

Today, the average American worker **doesn't keep** the same job for a long time. Young people change jobs often. Older people **don't like** to change jobs often. The average worker in America keeps a job for about five years.

Vocabulary
in Context

salary	He is a teacher. His **salary** is $55,000 per year.
wage	They work in a store. Their **wage** is $8 an hour.
complain	She doesn't like her job. She **complains** about it a lot.
mean	A good salary **means** a worker gets a lot of money each year.
average	Most workers don't stay at one job for a long time. The **average** worker changes jobs often.
day off	Tomorrow is Tuesday. It's my **day off.** I don't work on Tuesdays.
relax	We **relax** on Sundays. We don't work.
overtime	I don't like to work **overtime.** I don't like to work more than 40 hours.
keep	They **keep** their jobs for several years. They are at the same job for several years.

- All states need to have a minimum hourly wage. It's the law in America. But each state can decide to make the minimum wage higher.
- Workers usually get time and a half (50% more per hour) for overtime work.

Listening Activity

Listen to the sentences about the reading. Circle *true* or *false*.

EXAMPLE (TRUE)   FALSE

1. TRUE   FALSE   5. TRUE   FALSE
2. TRUE   FALSE   6. TRUE   FALSE
3. TRUE   FALSE   7. TRUE   FALSE
4. TRUE   FALSE

4.5 | Simple Present Tense—Negative Forms

Subject	Don't	Verb (Base Form)	Complement
I	don't	work	on Saturdays.
You	don't	live	near your work.
We	don't	enjoy	overtime work.
They	don't	spend	much money.
Those people	don't	get	wages.

Subject	Doesn't	Verb (Base Form)	Complement
He	doesn't	have	a full-time job.
She	doesn't	like	her job.
An American	doesn't	ask	about a person's salary.

Language Notes:

1. Compare the affirmative and negative forms.

    He **has** time. He **doesn't have** money.

    She **goes** to work on Friday. She **doesn't go** to work on Saturday.

    They **get** a wage. They **don't get** a salary.

2. The frequency words *hardly ever*, *never*, and *rarely* are not used with negative verbs. They have a negative meaning.

    We **hardly ever have** any days off.

    I **never work** on weekends.

EXERCISE 1 Fill in the blanks with the negative form of the verb in parentheses ( ).

EXAMPLE He ____*doesn't have*____ a part-time job.
                          (have)

1. Young people _____ their jobs a long time.
                          (keep)

2. Dorota _____ about her job.
                (complain)

3. You and I _____ a lot of money.
                    (make)

4. American workers _____ the same days off.
                              (have)

5. Simon _____ about his salary.
              (talk)

6. A day off _____ free time for some people.
                    (mean)

EXERCISE 2 Write a negative sentence with the words given.

EXAMPLES Simon works on Saturday. (on Wednesday)
Simon doesn't work on Wednesday.

Simon works on Saturday. (Many Americans)
Many Americans don't work on Saturday.

1. Simon gets a salary. (an hourly wage)

   _____

2. A *salary* means money for a year of work. (money for an hour of work)

   _____

3. Some people complain about long work hours. (Dorota and Simon)

   _____

4. Workers in most stores get two days off. (weekends off)

   _____

5. Halina works part-time. (40 hours a week)

   _____

6. Many Americans work overtime. (Simon and Dorota)

   _____

4.6 | Expressions of Time with the Simple Present Tense

Subject	Verb (+ Complement)	Time Expression
She	works doesn't work	eight hours a day. five days a week. every day. on the weekends.
We	work overtime don't work overtime	twice a week. once a month. on Tuesdays.
They	complain don't complain	every five minutes. all the time.

Language Note: Time expressions go at the end of the sentence. They never go before the base form.

EXERCISE 3 ABOUT YOU Write a sentence about you. Use the simple present tense—affirmative or negative—and an expression of time. Add extra information where possible.

EXAMPLE take the bus

I take the bus twice a day.   OR

I don't take the bus. I drive every day.

1. eat

   _____

2. work

   _____

3. have a day off

   _____

4. drive

   _____

5. do the laundry

   _____

6. come to this class

   _____

7. go to the supermarket

   _____

4.7 | Infinitives with Simple Present Verbs

We often use the infinitive form with simple present verbs. The infinitive form is always the same. Use infinitives after the following verbs: *want, need, like, expect,* and *try.*

Subject	Verb	Infinitive Form	Complement
I	like don't like	**to relax**	on the weekends.
He	wants doesn't want	**to take**	a day off.
She	expects doesn't expect	**to have**	a day off.
We	try don't try	**to do**	good work.
They	need don't need	**to work**	on Saturday.

EXERCISE 4   Fill in the blanks with the simple present + infinitive. Use affirmative or negative and the words in parentheses ( ).

EXAMPLES   We ___*don't expect to speak*___ our native language in this class.

                     (not expect/speak)

               We ___*expect to speak*___ English in this class.

                     (expect/speak)

1. Some people _____.

                (like/complain)

2. He _____ his job.

          (not want/leave)

3. We _____ a day off this week.

          (need/take)

4. Americans _____ every day.

            (not expect/work)

5. Dorota _____ on Sundays.

          (not like/work)

6. That young man always _____ a good job.

                (try/do)

EXERCISE 5 Write the sentences again. Add the verbs in parentheses ( ).

EXAMPLES She takes a day off on Sunday. (want)
She wants to take a day off on Sunday.

She doesn't take a day off on Sunday. (want)
She doesn't want to take a day off on Sunday.

1. That football team wins every game. (try)

   _____

2. The workers don't make a lot of money. (expect)

   _____

3. I don't complain about my job. (want)

   _____

4. Simon doesn't work overtime. (need)

   _____

EXERCISE 6 Fill in the blanks in the conversation with the simple present tense. Use the negative form of the verbs in parentheses ( ).

Irma: We have a day off tomorrow. Let's go to the museum.

Sara: I'm sorry. But I ___*don't have*___ time. I need to look for a new job.
           (example: have)

Irma: You have a job.

Sara: I know. But I _____ it. I _____ enough
                        (1. like)   *(2. work)*

   hours. And the job _____ enough money. My boss
                       (3. pay)

   _____ my work. It's not a good job for me.
    (4. like)

Irma: There's a job in my company. But it's only part-time.

Sara: Thanks, Irma, but I _____ to work part-time. I
                              (5. want)

   need a full-time job.

Irma: The Web is a good place to look. But most people

   _____ their jobs on Web sites. They hear about them
    (6. find)

   from other people. So ask all of your friends.

EXERCISE **7** ABOUT YOU Fill in the blanks with the simple present tense of the verbs in parentheses ( ). Use the affirmative or negative form. Write **true** sentences about work in your home town or country. Read your sentences to the class.

EXAMPLE The average worker in my home town ___*doesn't work*___ every day.
(work)

1. A worker _____ two days off every week.
(get)

2. Most people _____ more than eight hours a day at work.
(spend)

3. A company _____ more money for overtime work.
(pay)

4. People _____ to work overtime.
(like)

5. Most people _____ about their jobs.
(complain)

6. My country _____ a minimum hourly wage for workers.
(have)

7. The average worker _____ a part-time job on days off.
(take)

8. Workers _____ four weeks off each year with pay.
(expect/get)

9. People _____ on vacation on their weeks off.
(go)

10. The average worker _____ jobs often.
(change)

11. The average worker _____ at the same job for a long time.
(stay)

12. Most women in my hometown _____.
(work)

LESSON 3

GRAMMAR

Yes/No Questions in the Simple Present Tense

CONTEXT

Eating Customs

Before You Read

Circle *yes* or *no*.

1. Do you like American food? YES NO
2. Do you eat in American restaurants? YES NO

EATING CUSTOMS

Halina: It's 1:30. It's early. **Do Americans** usually **have** lunch at this time?

Dorota: One-thirty is late. Lunch hours usually begin at 11 a.m. Americans usually have an hour for lunch. **Do you want to order** a sandwich, Halina?

Halina: Yes, I do. I'm hungry. Look. That man has a sandwich. What is it?

Dorota: It's a mushroom sandwich.

Halina: **Does it have** meat with the mushroom?

Dorota: I don't think so. Maybe the man's a vegetarian. Some people don't eat meat.

Halina: **Do Americans** often **eat** in restaurants?

Dorota: Yes, they do. They're very busy. They don't have time to cook every meal. Sometimes they go out. Sometimes they order from restaurants.

Halina: **Do restaurants deliver** food to your home?

Dorota: Yes, some do. And many restaurants have "take-out" food. They prepare the food for you. You take it home to eat. Supermarkets have prepared food too. It's in the deli section. They have hot and cold food. Sometimes people eat the food in the supermarkets at special tables. Most people take home prepared food. Prepared food is very popular.

Halina: **Does prepared food cost** more?

Dorota: Yes, it does. But it's very convenient.

Vocabulary
in Context

mushroom(s)	I like **mushrooms.** They are very good for your health.
vegetarian	He's a **vegetarian.** He doesn't eat meat.
order	She wants to **order** a sandwich. She asks for a mushroom sandwich.
deliver	That restaurant **delivers** pizza. Someone brings it to your house.
take-out	Let's order **take-out.** We take the food home to eat.
deli	Let's go to the **deli** section. They have sandwiches there.
prepared food	**Prepared food** is very popular. People don't need to cook it.
convenient	Prepared food is **convenient.** It's easy because we don't have to cook it.

Did You Know?

- About 10 million Americans are vegetarians. Most are young women in cities.
- The U.S. has two times more women vegetarians than men.

Listening Activity Listen to the statements about the conversation. Circle *true* or *false*.

EXAMPLE   (TRUE)   FALSE

1. TRUE   FALSE   5. TRUE   FALSE
2. TRUE   FALSE   6. TRUE   FALSE
3. TRUE   FALSE   7. TRUE   FALSE
4. TRUE   FALSE

4.8 | *Yes / No* Questions in the Simple Present Tense

Do	Subject	Verb (Base Form)	Complement	Short Answer
Do	you	**like**	American food?	No, I don't.
Do	we	**want**	prepared food today?	No, we don't.
Do	they	**enjoy**	vegetarian food?	Yes, they do.
Do	vegetarians	**eat**	meat?	No, they don't.
Does	Subject	Verb (Base Form)	Complement	Short Answer
Does	he	**go**	to a restaurant for lunch?	Yes, he does.
Does	she	**take**	a long lunch hour?	No, she doesn't.
Does	this restaurant	**have**	take-out food?	Yes, it does.

EXERCISE 1   Fill in the blanks with *do* or *does*. Then write a short answer to each question.

EXAMPLE   _____Does_____ your wife cook at home?

Yes, she does. _____

1. _____ vegetarians eat meat?

   _____

2. _____ some restaurants deliver to your home?

   _____

3. _____ a mushroom sandwich have meat?

_____

4. _____ supermarkets have deli sections?

_____

5. _____ the deli section have hot and cold food?

_____

6. _____ the American lunch hour usually start at 11 a.m.?

_____

7. _____ American workers take two hours for lunch?

_____

EXERCISE 2 Complete each short conversation with a question in the simple present tense. Use the words given.

EXAMPLE A: Many Americans eat lunch outside the home. (eat in restaurants)

B: *Do Americans eat lunch in restaurants?* _____

1. A: He likes meat. (like mushrooms)

   B: _____

2. A: She buys food in that supermarket. (buy prepared food)

   B: _____

3. A: That restaurant has take-out food. (have vegetarian food)

   B: _____

4. A: You go to lunch early. (go at 11:00 a.m.)

   B: _____

5. A: Halina and Dorota want to order some lunch. (want to order sandwiches)

   B: _____

6. A: This restaurant delivers pizza. (deliver sandwiches)

   B: _____

7. A: Americans eat prepared food. (eat it in the supermarket)

   B: _____

EXERCISE **3**   Complete the conversation with the correct question from the box.

Do you work during the week?	Does the job pay well?
Do you deliver the pizzas?	Do you use your car?

Victor: I have a new part-time job. I work for Joe's Pizza.

1. Simon: _____?

   Victor: Yes, I do. I deliver them all over the city.

2. Simon: _____?

   Victor: No, I don't. I work on the weekends.

3. Simon: _____?

   Victor: No, I don't. Joe's has a car with "Joe's Pizza" on it.

4. Simon: _____?

   Victor: No, it doesn't. But people often give me extra money for the delivery.

   Simon: We call that money a "tip."

EXERCISE **4**   ABOUT YOU Find a partner. Ask your partner a *yes/no* question with the words given. Give short answers and add information where possible. Then tell the class about your partner's answers.

EXAMPLE   you/like to eat in restaurants
Student 1: Do you like to eat in restaurants?
Student 2: Yes, I do. I like to eat in Chinese restaurants.
Student 1: Maria likes to eat in Chinese restaurants.

1. you / like pizza

2. you / work in a restaurant

3. you / have a part-time job

4. you / eat only vegetarian food

5. you / sometimes order take-out food

6. you / eat lunch at home

7. someone / cook for you

8. restaurants in your country / deliver

9. supermarkets in your country / have deli sections

10. many people in your country / eat vegetarian food

EXERCISE 5 Shafia and Ali are at Halina and Peter's house for dinner. Fill in the blanks in their conversation with a *yes/no* question in the simple present tense.

Shafia: Halina, this is a delicious meal. _____*Do you cook*_____
(example: you/cook)

like this every day? _____ time?
(1. you/have)

Halina: Not exactly. _____ good?
(2. the food/taste)

Ali: The meat is very good. _____ a special sauce?
(3. it/have)

Halina: Well . . . yes. But . . .

Shafia: I like the carrots. There's something different about them.

_____ orange in them?
(4. they/have)

Halina: Yes, I think so. I'm happy that you like them.

Ali: _____ Halina?
(5. you/like to cook)

Peter: Tell them about the meal, Halina.

Halina: Well . . . it's all from the supermarket!

Shafia: Of course. But you're the cook. And it's all delicious.

Halina: No, I'm not the cook. It's all prepared food.

Ali: _____ hot food like this?
(6. the supermarket/prepare)

Halina: Yes, it does.

Shafia: _____ prepared food often?
(7. you and Peter/eat)

Halina: No, we don't. But sometimes it's very convenient.

sauce

LESSON 4

GRAMMAR

Information Questions in the Simple Present Tense
Question Words as Subjects

CONTEXT

Exercise

Before You Read

1. Do you exercise every day?
2. What kind of exercise do you do?

park   sneakers   gym   bicycle   office building

EXERCISE

Halina: Look at that woman with a business suit and sneakers!

Dorota: That's Louisa. I know her. She walks during her lunch hour. Some Americans use their lunch hours for exercise.

Halina: **Where does she walk** in the winter?

Dorota: Maybe she goes to a gym. The building next door is a gym. Maybe her office building has a gym.

Halina: **What do you mean?**

Dorota: Some office buildings have gyms inside for their workers. They're free.

Halina: That's very interesting. I see a lot of people on bicycles too. Bicycles are great exercise. But **why does that man have** strange clothes?

Dorota: He works on his bicycle. He takes mail from one office to another here in the city. He gets a lot of exercise every day!

Halina: **Why do so many Americans exercise?**

Dorota: Most Americans don't exercise. But some do. Many people have desk jobs. They sit all day. So they try to exercise a little every day.

Halina: **What kind of exercise do you do,** Dorota?

Dorota: I walk. It's great exercise for me. I stay healthy this way.

Halina: **Where do you walk?**

Dorota: I go to a park near my house.

Halina: **How often do you exercise?**

Dorota: I try to walk every day. But I don't always have time.

Vocabulary in Context

sneaker(s)	I wear **sneakers,** not regular shoes, for exercise.
gym	I go to a **gym.** I exercise there.
next door	The building **next door** is a gym.
ride a bicycle	I have a **bicycle.** I **ride** it to work.
desk job	He has a **desk job.** He works at a desk all day.
exercise (n.) exercise (v.)	They walk for **exercise.** Americans don't **exercise** a lot.
park	A **park** is a good place for exercise.
during	She often walks **during** her lunch hour.
healthy	Dorota is **healthy.** She's not sick.

Did You Know?

- We need only one 30-minute walk or two 15-minute walks each day for good health.
- Exercise helps lower stress levels.

Listening Activity Listen to the statements about the conversation. Circle *true* or *false*.

EXAMPLE   TRUE   (FALSE)

1. TRUE   FALSE   4. TRUE   FALSE
2. TRUE   FALSE   5. TRUE   FALSE
3. TRUE   FALSE   6. TRUE   FALSE

4.9 | Information Questions in the Simple Present Tense

Question Word	*Do*	Subject	Verb (Base Form)	Short Answer
How often	**do**	you	**exercise?**	Three times a week.
Why	**do**	we	**exercise?**	Because we want to stay healthy.
Where	**do**	they	**exercise?**	In a gym.
When	**do**	they	**exercise?**	In the morning.
How	**does**	he	**exercise?**	He walks.
Question Word	***Does***	**Subject**	**Verb (Base Form)**	**Short Answer**
What kind of exercise	**does**	she	**do?**	She rides a bicycle.
What	**does**	"bike"	**mean?**	It means bicycle.
How much	**does**	a bike	**cost?**	It costs about $200.
Who	**does**	Dorota	**know?**	She knows Louisa.
How many days	**does**	Dorota	**exercise?**	She exercises seven days a week.

Language Notes:

1. We use *because* with answers to *why* questions.
2. When we say *how often*, we want an exact number of times.
3. We use the simple present with *mean* and *cost*.

EXERCISE **1**   Fill in the correct question word in each short conversation. Use: *what, who, when, where, how, why, what kind of, how many,* and *how often.* The underlined words are the answers to the questions.

EXAMPLE   A: _How often_ does she ride her bicycle?

B: She rides her bicycle every day.

1. A: _____ does *gym* mean?

   B: It means a place for exercise.

2. A: _____ do they walk every day?

   B: Because it's good exercise.

3. A: _____ hours do they walk every day?

   B: They walk for three hours every day.

4. A: _____ shoes does Louisa have?

   B: She has sneakers.

5. A: _____ do some people get to work?

   B: They ride their bicycles.

6. A: _____ does Halina see in the street?

   B: She sees some people on bicycles.

7. A: _____ does Dorota walk in the park?

   B: She walks four or five days a week.

EXERCISE **2**   Write questions with the words given. Write an answer to each question. Use the ideas from the conversation.

EXAMPLE   what / Halina / ask Dorota

What does Halina ask Dorota?

She asks Dorota about exercise in the U.S.

1. what kind of exercise / Dorota / do

   _____

   _____

2. where / Dorota / exercise

   _____

   _____

3. when / some office workers / exercise

_____

_____

4. what / some office buildings / have for their workers

_____

_____

5. why / some office workers / exercise

_____

_____

6. what / mean / "bike"

_____

_____

EXERCISE 3 Complete the short conversation with a question in the simple present tense. Use the question word given.

EXAMPLE **A:** She walks for exercise. (how often)

B: _How often does she walk?_ _____

1. A: She likes to wear sneakers. (why)

B: _____

2. A: She has a day off each week. (when)

B: _____

3. A: I have some new shoes. (what kind of)

B: _____

4. A: They stay healthy. (how)

B: _____

5. A: She goes to the gym in the winter. (how often)

B: _____

6. A: Halina sees some friends in the street. (how many)

B: _____

7. A: People wear special clothes for exercise. (what kind of)

B: _____

4.10 | Question Words as Subjects

Do not use *do/does* when the question word is a subject.

Question Word (Subject)	Verb (Base Form or -s Form)	Complement	Short Answer
Who	**wants**	a sandwich?	I do.
Who	**works**	in that company?	We all do.
What kind of people	**exercise**	here?	Office workers.
Which company	**has**	a gym for workers?	My company does.
Which workers	**exercise**	during their lunch hours?	Louisa and two of her friends do.
How many people	**wear**	sneakers to exercise?	Everybody does.

Language Note: *Who* questions are singular. Answers can be singular or plural.

EXERCISE **4** Use the question words in parentheses ( ) as subjects. Write a question about each statement.

EXAMPLE   Somebody needs a job. (who)
Who needs a job?

1. Somebody wants to exercise. (who)

   _____

2. Some jobs pay well. (what kind of)

   _____

3. Some people ride their bicycles to work. (how many)

   _____

4. Some people take three days off a week. (who)

   _____

5. Some people exercise during their lunch hours. (which)

   _____

6. Some workers in my company sit all day. (how many)

   _____

7. Some exercise helps your heart. (what kind of)

   _____

EXERCISE **5** Match the questions on the left with the answers on the right. Put the letter of the answer on the line next to the question.

EXAMPLE   Who walks five days a week? __C__

Questions

1. Where do business people work? _____

2. How often does she walk to work? _____

3. How does he exercise? _____

4. What does *gym* mean? _____.

5. Who do you exercise with? _____

6. When does he ride his bicycle? _____

7. What do they wear to the office? _____

8. Why does she go to the gym? _____

9. What kind of shoes does he wear to the gym? _____

10. How many people exercise during their lunch hour? _____

11. What kind of people use their bicycles for work? _____

Answers

A. business suits

B. sneakers

C. Dorota ✓

D. Usually young people. They deliver packages.

E. in offices

F. He plays soccer.

G. my brother

H. a place for exercise

I. in the evening

J. twice a week

K. to exercise

L. about 20 from our office

EDITING ADVICE

1. Don't use the *-s* form after *does* or *doesn't*.

   She doesn't ~~has~~ ^{have} a new job.　　　Where does she ~~works~~?

2. Don't put time expressions before the verb.

   We (every day) go to work.

3. Use *do / does* in all questions except subject questions.

   What ~~you want~~ ^{do you want} to do?　　　Who ~~does want~~ ^{wants} to go to the gym?

4. Use the correct word order in questions.

   Where does (work) your friend?

5. Use the normal question word order with *mean* and *cost*.

   What ~~means~~ "Super Bowl?" ^{does "Super Bowl" mean?}

6. Use frequency words in the correct place.

   He goes (always) to the gym.

EDITING QUIZ

Find the mistakes with the underlined words, and correct them. Not every sentence has a mistake. If the sentence is correct, write *C*.

EXAMPLE　　How much ~~costs a grill~~? ^{does a grill cost?}

1. She <u>once a week</u> likes to work overtime.

2. He <u>doesn't likes</u> to work overtime.

3. <u>What he wants</u> to cook on the grill?

4. Does he <u>enjoys</u> the museum in his city?

5. How often <u>do they eat</u> mushrooms?

6. <u>What means</u> "gym"?

7. How many people <u>do want to work</u> overtime?

8. We <u>eat never</u> in a restaurant.

1. What did you learn in this unit? Write three sentences in your notebook about each of these topics:
   - Free-time activities in the U.S.
   - Work in the U.S.
   - Food and exercise in the U.S.

2. Write three questions you still have about work and free-time activities in America.

EXPANSION ACTIVITIES

Writing Activity

Rewrite the following paragraph about Nina in your notebook. Change *I* to *she*. Change the first *she* to *Nina*.

> I live in Chicago. I like the city. Why do I like it? Because it's wonderful in the summer time. I often go to a big park downtown. It has concerts every Thursday evening. I don't pay for these concerts. They're free for all the people. I like to visit Lake Michigan. It has many free public beaches. But the water is cold. I don't swim in June or July. I swim only in August. I also visit a beautiful park on the lake. Sometimes I have dinner on one of the big ships there. I don't do that often. It's expensive. I often invite friends to visit this lovely city.

EXAMPLE   *Nina lives in Chicago.*

Outside Activities

1. Go to the deli section in a supermarket near your house. Find some prepared food that you like. Tell the class what it is. How much does the food cost?

2. Find a pizza restaurant near your house or this school. Get a take-out menu from the restaurant. Find a meal you like. Find the total price. Tell the class about it.

3. Look for a movie in a theater near you. Find the price of a regular ticket. Find the price of a ticket before 5 or 6 p.m.

Internet Activities

1. Find the Web site for your city. Look under *events* to find some fun activities in your city this week. Look under *museums* or *parks* in your city to find special activities there. Tell the class about them.

2. Search the words *United States minimum wage*. Find the minimum wage for your state. Compare it to the national minimum wage.

UNIT

5

GRAMMAR
Modal Verbs: *Can, Should, Have To*

CONTEXT
Driving

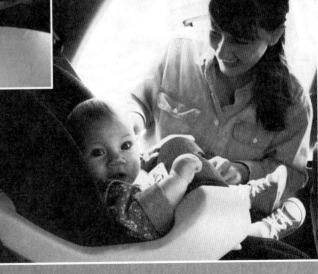

LESSON 1

GRAMMAR

Can

Should

Have To

CONTEXT

Getting a Driver's License

Before You Read

Circle *yes* or *no*.

1. Can you drive? YES   NO

2. Do you have a driver's license from this state? YES   NO

GETTING A DRIVER'S LICENSE

Simon's son, Ed, wants to learn to drive. He is 15 years old.

Ed: Dad, I want to drive.

Simon: You **have to get** a learner's permit first.

Ed: You **can help** me with that.

Simon: No, I **can't.** In this state, drivers under age 18 **have to take** a driver's training class at school. It's the law.

Ed: A class takes a long time. I can learn faster with you.

Simon: No, you **can't.** It takes a long time to learn to drive. You **shouldn't be** in a hurry. First you **have to pass** two tests: a vision test and a written test. The written test is about the rules of driving in this state. You have to study 30 hours in the classroom. It's the law.

Ed: And then I **can get** my license. I **don't have to wait** anymore.

Simon: No. You **can get** a learner's permit. Then you **have to practice** in the car. You **should practice** many hours in a car. In this state, you **have to practice** at least six hours. And you **have to wait** three months. Then you **can take** the driving test.

Ed: Then I **can get** my license. And I **can drive** with my friends.

Simon: Not exactly.

Ed: What do you mean?

Simon: New drivers under the age of 17 don't get a full license in this state. You **have to drive** with an adult driver at night. You **can have** only one other teenager in the car. And you **can't drive** at all from 11 p.m. to 6 a.m. This law saves a lot of lives every year.

Vocabulary in Context

permit	A **permit** means the law lets you do something.
then	First I have to study. **Then** I can go out.
It takes time	**It takes** a long **time** to be a good driver.
training	People learn to drive in a driver's **training** class.
in a hurry	Ed wants his license now. He's **in a hurry.**
vision test	A **vision test** checks a person's eyes.
written test	We use pencil and paper for a **written test.**
pass a test	When you **pass** the tests, you can get the permit.
at least	He has to practice **at least** six hours. He can practice six hours or more.
law(s)	The government makes **laws.** Laws keep citizens safe.
without	He can't drive **without** a license.

- Car crashes are the number one cause of death for people ages 16 to 19. These teenagers have four times more deaths from car crashes than drivers over age 20.
- Most accidents happen at night with friends in the car.

Listening Activity

Listen to the sentences about the conversation. Circle *true* or *false*.

EXAMPLE   TRUE   (FALSE)

1. TRUE FALSE		5. TRUE FALSE	
2. TRUE FALSE		6. TRUE FALSE	
3. TRUE FALSE		7. TRUE FALSE	
4. TRUE FALSE			

5.1 | *Can*

We use *can* to show: ability, permission, or possibility.

Subject	*Can*	Verb (Base Form)	Complement
I She Simon It We You They	**can** **cannot** **can't**	help	him.

Language Note: We often use **can't** to show rules or laws.

You **can't** park at a bus stop. It's against the law.

Pronunciation Note: In affirmative statements, we usually pronounce *can*/kən/. In negative statements, we pronounce *can't*/kænt/. It is hard to hear the final **t,** so we use the vowel sound and stress to tell the difference between *can* and *can't*. Listen to your teacher pronounce these sentences:

I *can* go. [accent on *go*]

I *can't* go. [accent on *can't*]

EXERCISE 1 Fill in the blanks with *can* or *can't*. Use the ideas from the conversation.

EXAMPLE   Ed _____*can't*_____ drive now.

1. Drivers with a learner's permit _____ get a license after three months in Ed's state.

2. Ed _____ get his permit without a driver's training class.

3. Drivers under age 17 _____ drive late at night in Ed's state.

4. Ed _____ take the driver's training class now.

5. Simon _____ help Ed practice in the car.

6. Ed _____ get a full license at age 16.

7. Ed _____ drive with a lot of his friends in the car.

8. Ed _____ drive without a full license.

5.2 | *Should*

We use *should* when we give advice or make a suggestion.			
Subject	***Should***	**Verb (Base Form)**	**Complement**
I He She We You They	**should should not shouldn't**	take	the test today.

EXERCISE 2 Give advice in each conversation. Use *should* or *shouldn't* and the words in parentheses ( ).

EXAMPLE   A: I have my written test tomorrow.

B: _____*You should read*_____ the rules of the road again tonight.
　　　　　　　(you/read)

1. A: My car is dirty.

B: _____ it today!
　　　(you/wash)

2. **A:** Drivers with a learner's permit don't have much practice.

 B: _____ .
   (they/drive too fast)

3. **A:** Ed wants to learn to drive.

 B: _____ in a hurry.
   (he/be)

4. **A:** Ed wants to be a safe driver.

 B: _____ a lot with a good driver.
   (he/practice)

5. **A:** Ed doesn't know the driving laws in his state.

 B: _____ them before the written test.
   (he/learn)

6. **A:** Many cars are on the roads from 4 p.m. to 7 p.m.

 B: Then _____ on those busy roads.
   (you/drive)

7. **A:** I don't have the book of driving rules, and I need to check something.

 B: _____ online. The information is
   (you/look)

 on the state Web site.

5.3 | *Have To*

Have to shows necessity.

Subject	*Have to*	Verb (Base Form)	Complement
She Your teacher Simon	**has to** **doesn't have to**	take	a driver's training class.
I You We They	**have to** **don't have to**		

Pronunciation Note: In normal speech, we pronounce *have to* /hæftə/. We pronounce *has to* /hæstə/. Listen to your teacher pronounce the following sentences in normal speech:

 We *have to* take the test.   She *has to* drive safely.

 They *have to* follow the rules of the road.

Language Note: In the affirmative, **have to** shows laws or strong necessity.

 Ed **has to** get a learner's permit.

In the negative, **have to** means not necessary.

 Simon **doesn't have to** work on Saturday.

EXERCISE 3 Fill in the blanks with an affirmative or negative form of *have to*. Use the verbs in parentheses ( ) and the ideas from the conversation.

EXAMPLE Ed _____*has to take*_____ a driver's training class.
$\qquad$ (take)

1. Simon _____ a learner's permit.
$\qquad$ (get)

2. All drivers _____ the vision and written tests.
$\qquad$ (pass)

3. Ed _____ at least six hours to take the driving test.
$\qquad$ (practice)

4. People over age 18 _____ a driver's training class.
$\qquad$ (take)

5. An adult driver _____ with drivers under age 18
$\qquad$ (be)
during the day.

6. All drivers _____ driver's licenses.
$\qquad$ (have)

7. Simon _____ Ed the driving rules.
$\qquad$ (teach)

EXERCISE 4 ABOUT YOU Write true sentences about your English class. Fill in the blanks with the affirmative or negative form of *have to*.

EXAMPLE We _____*have to speak*_____ English in class.
$\qquad$ (speak)

1. We _____ homework for every class.
$\qquad$ (do)

2. We _____ homework to the teacher
$\qquad$ (give)
every day.

3. We _____ in the same seat every day.
$\qquad$ (sit)

4. We _____ a pen to write our exercises.
$\qquad$ (use)

5. We _____ our book to class every day.
$\qquad$ (bring)

6. The teacher _____ all our exercises at home.
   (check)

7. We _____ a final test at the end of the semester.
   (take)

8. The teacher _____ us all an "A."
   (give)

EXERCISE **5**   Look at the following road signs from Ed's rule book. Write an affirmative or a negative sentence about each sign. Write two sentences if possible. Use affirmative and negative forms of *can*, *should*, or *have to*.

> SPEED
> LIMIT
> **55**
> MINIMUM
> **45**

EXAMPLES   *Drivers can't go over 55 miles per hour.*

   Drivers have to go at least 45 miles per hour.

1. _____
   _____
   _____

2. _____
   _____
   _____

3. _____
   _____
   _____

4. _____
   _____
   _____

DO NOT ENTER

5. _____
_____
_____

ONE WAY

6. _____
_____
_____

WRONG WAY

7. _____
_____
_____

8. _____
_____
_____

EXERCISE 6 ABOUT YOU With a partner, write about what you can or can't do in this class or in this school.

EXAMPLES We can _write in pen or pencil in this class._

We can't _eat in class in this school._

1. We can _____
2. We can't _____
3. We should _____
4. We shouldn't _____
5. We have to _____
6. We don't have to _____

EXERCISE 7 Read the following conversations. Fill in the blanks with the affirmative or negative form of *can*, *should*, or *have to* and the verb in parentheses ( ).

EXAMPLE   **A:** I don't have a car.

       B: Don't worry. You ___*can use*___ my car today.
                           (use)

1. **A:** I don't like to drive.

 B: That's OK. You _____ the bus.
                            (take)

2. **A:** Where are your keys?

 B: They're in the car.

 A: You _____ your keys in the car. Someone may
                       (leave)
 take them.

3. **A:** I have a new bicycle for your son.

 B: That's great, but he _____ a bicycle yet.
                          (ride)

4. **A:** Your car is very dirty.

 B: I know. I _____ a car wash today, but I'm
                      (get)
 too busy.

5. **A:** Let's walk to work today.

 B: We _____. We don't have time. We
                     (walk)

 _____ at work in 30 minutes.
              (be)

6. **A:** I don't like to take the bus.

 B: I know. But we _____ today. We need to
                     (take)
 fix the car.

7. **A:** My son wants to get his driver's license.

 B: He _____ classes with the new driving
                  (take)
 school. The teachers are very good there.

EXERCISE 8 Fill in the blanks in the conversations with the correct verbs from the box.

CONVERSATION A: Ed is asking Simon about his friend from Mexico.

doesn't have to get	should study	can drive
has to take	has to get	can use

Ed: Dad, one of my friends has an international driver's license.

He _____ it to drive in this state, right?
(1)

Simon: Yes, he can. But he _____ with an international
(2)

license for three months. Then he _____
(3)

a new driver's license for this state.

Ed: What about the learner's permit?

Simon: He _____ a learner's permit. But he
(4)

_____ all three of the tests. And he
(5)

_____ the rules of the road carefully. They are
(6)

very different from the rules in Mexico.

CONVERSATION B: The teacher, Mr. Brown, is talking to students in the high school driver's training class.

have to wear	can't see	shouldn't worry

Mr. Brown: Today's class is about the tests for your learner's permit.
Does anyone have a question? Karl?

Karl: I'm worried about the vision test. I _____
(1)

very well.

Mr. Brown: You _____. You can take the test with
(2)

your glasses on. But then you _____ your
(3)

glasses in the car too. It's the law.

LESSON 2

GRAMMAR

Modal Verbs: *Yes/No* Questions with *Can, Should,* and *Have To*

Information Questions with Modal Verbs

Question Words as Subjects

CONTEXT

Car Safety for Children

Before You Read

1. Where should children sit in a car?

2. Do you have a child in your family? What kind of car seat does the child use?

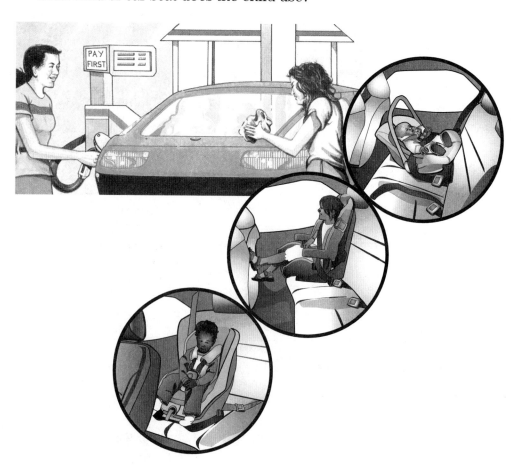

CAR SAFETY FOR CHILDREN

Dorota and Halina are on the way to an outlet mall in another city. Halina asks Dorota about car seats for her daughter, Anna.

Halina: This is my first trip to an outlet mall. **Can I get** a new car seat for Anna there? She is too big for her old infant seat now. And she's still too small for a seat belt.

Dorota: Sure. And things aren't so expensive at the outlet mall.

Halina: **What kind of car seat should I get?**

Dorota: Well, she's two now. There are many different kinds of seats for older babies. We can look in several stores.

Halina: **How long does Anna have to be** in a car seat, Dorota?

Dorota: In this state, children have to be in a car seat until age eight or 57 inches tall.

Halina: **Where should I put** Anna's seat? **Can I put** it on the front passenger seat?

Dorota: No. Anna shouldn't be in the front seat. The air bag can hurt children. They should sit in the back seat until age 12.

Dorota: Halina, I have to stop for gas. Here's a gas station.

Halina: I can pay, Dorota. **Do we have to pay first?**

Dorota: Yes, the sign says "Pay First." But don't worry, Halina. I can put it on my credit card. I can pay right here at the pump.

Halina: **Should I wash** the windows?

Dorota: OK. You can wash the windows. And I can pump the gas.

Halina: **Where can I get** some water? I'm thirsty.

Dorota: Right here! This gas station has a store.

Vocabulary in Context

trip	We are in the car. We are on a **trip** out of town.
on the way	I'm **on the way** home. I'm almost home.
outlet mall	People can buy things cheaper at **outlet malls.** Outlet malls are sometimes very large with many stores.
air bag(s)	An **air bag** helps in an accident. It protects the people in the front seats.
infant	That baby is only three months old. She's an **infant.**
seatbelt	Everyone has to wear a **seatbelt** in a car. It's the law.
passenger	A **passenger** sits next to the driver.
hurt	In an accident, an airbag can **hurt** a small child.
pump (v) **pump (n)**	We have to **pump** our own gas. We can pay at the **pump** with a credit card.

- You can get information about car seats on the Internet or at a neighborhood police station.
- Tickets for not putting a child in a car seat can be up to $100 in some states.

🎧 Listening Activity

Listen to each statement about the conversation. Circle *true* or *false*.

EXAMPLE (TRUE)   FALSE

1. TRUE   FALSE   5. TRUE   FALSE

2. TRUE   FALSE   6. TRUE   FALSE

3. TRUE   FALSE   7. TRUE   FALSE

4. TRUE   FALSE

5.4 | Yes/No Questions with *Can, Should,* and *Have To*

Modal Verb	Subject	Verb (Base Form)	Complement	Short Answer
Can	I	get	some water?	Yes, you can.
Should	we	pay	inside?	No, we shouldn't.

Language Note: Question forms and short answers with *can* and *should* are the same for all subjects.

Do/Does	Subject	Have To	Verb (Base Form)	Complement	Short Answer
Does	he	**have to**	get	gas now?	Yes, he does.
Does	she	**have to**	pay	in cash?	No, she doesn't.
Do	I	**have to**	pump	the gas?	Yes, you do.
Do	we	**have to**	pay	inside?	No, we don't.

Language Note: Use *do/does* to make questions with *have to*.

EXERCISE 1 Write an affirmative or negative short answer for each question. Use the ideas from the conversation.

EXAMPLE Does Dorota have to get gas?

_____*Yes, she does.*_____

1. Should Halina put Anna's car seat in the passenger seat?

_____

2. Can airbags hurt children?

_____

3. Does Dorota have to pay in cash for her gas?

_____

4. Do people have to pump their own gas at the gas station?

_____

5. Does Halina have to pay for the gas?

_____

6. Should young children sit in the back seat of the car?

_____

7. Can parents hold their babies in a car?

_____

EXERCISE 2 Fill in the blanks to make *yes/no* questions. Use the phrases from the column on the right. Write the questions on the blank.

EXAMPLE ___*Can I pay*___ with a credit card here?   Can I pay ✓

1. _____ for the gas?   Should we pay

2. _____ to the outlet mall?   Can I put

3. _____ the car seat in the front?   Does everyone have to use

4. _____ in the back seat?   Can we go

5. _____ first?   Should I pump

6. _____ a seatbelt?   Do they have to sit

EXERCISE **3** Match the statements on the left with a possible question on the right. The first one is done as an example.

1. The baby is only six months old. Can you go with me?

2. She's on the way to Should she wash them?
   another city.
   Can I hold her in the car?

3. She's 10 years old. Does she have to stop for gas?

4. She needs a new car seat. Should we try another gas
   station?
5. The car windows are dirty.
   Does she have to sit in a car
6. I want to take a trip. seat?

7. Gas here is expensive. Can she put it in the front seat?

EXERCISE **4** ABOUT YOU Ask your partner about people and customs in his/her native country. Use the words given. Your partner can give a short answer.

EXAMPLE _____Can people buy_____ food and drinks at gas stations? *Yes, they can.*
        (people/can/buy)

1. _____ their own gas at gas stations?
   (people/have to/pump)

2. _____ in special car seats?
   (children/have to/sit)

3. _____ a small child in a car?
   (a mother/can/hold)

4. _____ in the front?
   (children/can/sit)

5. _____ a seatbelt?
   (a driver/have to/use)

6. _____ for their gas at the pump?
   (people/can/pay)

7. _____ for gas with cash?
   (people/have to/pay)

5.5 | Information Questions with Modal Verbs

Can/Should

Question Word	Modal	Subject	Verb (Base Form)	Complement	Short Answer
Where	**can**	she	get	a car seat?	At a department store.
How long	**should**	children	sit	in the back?	Until age 12.
How	**can**	parents	keep	their children safe in a car?	They can put them in a car seat.
Which car seat	**should**	we	use	for a small baby?	An infant seat.

Have To

Question Word	Do/ Does	Subject	Have To	Verb (Base Form)	Complement	Short Answer
Where	**does**	your son	**have to**	sit?		In the back seat.
How much	**do**	we	**have to**	pay	for a car seat?	About $75.

EXERCISE **5** Answer each question. Use the ideas from the reading.

EXAMPLE How can people pay for gas?

They can pay with a credit card or cash.

1. When can a child sit in the front passenger seat?

_____

2. Why does a small child have to sit in the back?

_____

3. Why does Halina have to get a new car seat for Anna?

_____

4. How long does a child have to sit in a car seat?

_____

5. What kind of seat should Halina buy?

_____

6. Where can people pay for gas at the gas station?

_____

7. Why does Dorota have to stop at a gas station?

_____

EXERCISE 6 Ask questions about each statement using the question words given.

EXAMPLE Halina has to put Anna's car seat in the back.

Why _____ *does Halina have to put the car seat in the back* _____ ?

1. They have to stop for gas on their trip.

How often _____ ?

2. She should drive slowly.

Why _____ ?

3. An air bag can hurt small children.

How _____ ?

4. Simon has to buy some things for his car.

How many things _____ ?

5. You can use my car today.

How long _____ ?

6. You should get a better car seat for your daughter.

Why _____ ?

7. We have to pay first at this gas station.

Where _____ ?

EXERCISE 7 Complete each short conversation with a question. Use the words given.

EXAMPLE A: Please get in the car.

B: _____ *Where should we sit?* _____

(example: where/we/should sit)

1. **A:** There's child safety information on the Web.

   B: _____
   (which Web site/I/should check)

2. **A:** She doesn't have a car seat.

   B: _____
   (where/she/can buy a good one)

3. **A:** Their son is five years old.

   B: _____
   (which car seat/they/have to get for him)

4. **A:** Car seats have different prices.

   B: _____
   (how much/we/should spend)

5. **A:** Your seatbelt is broken.

   B: _____
   (how/I/can fix it)

6. **A:** That new driver is only 17 years old.

   B: _____
   (when/he/have to drive with an adult)

5.6 | Question Words as Subjects

Question Word (Subject)	Modal Verb	Verb (Base Form)	Complement	Short Answer
Who	**should**	pay	for the gas?	Dorota should.
What	**can**	happen	to the baby in the front seat?	The airbag can hurt her in an accident.
How many new drivers	**have to**	take	the written test today?	Only three.
Which drivers	**have to**	get	limited licenses?	All drivers 17 and under.

EXERCISE 8 Ask a question for each answer. Use the following question words as subjects: *who, which, how many,* or *what.* The underlined words are the answer.

EXAMPLE <u>Who has to buy a car seat?</u>

<u>Halina</u> has to buy a car seat.

1. _____

   The gas station <u>on my street</u> can give us the best price for gas.

2. _____

   <u>Nobody</u> should hold a child in a car.

3. _____

   <u>Ten</u> people have to take a trip today.

4. _____

   <u>Airbags</u> can be dangerous for children in a car.

5. _____

   Drivers <u>under age 17</u> have to drive with an adult at night.

6. _____

   <u>Halina</u> should buy some water.

EXERCISE 9 Fill in the conversation with one of the expressions from the box below.

| when does he have to take | can you put | he should practice |
| we can stop | I have to take | Ed should learn |

Marta and Simon talk about Ed's driving practice.

Marta: _____ some gas in the car for me today?
                    (1)

Simon: Sure. _____ Ed out for driving practice today.
                     (2)

   _____ at the gas station. _____
        (3)   (4)

   how to pump gas too.

Marta: _____ the driving test?
                    (5)

Simon: In just three weeks!

Marta: Then _____ a lot. He doesn't have much time.
                    (6)

EDITING ADVICE

1. Always use the base form after *can*, *should*, and *have to*.
    drive
    She can ~~drives~~ the car.

2. Don't use *to* after *can* and *should*.

    She can't ~~to~~ sit in the front seat.

3. Use the correct word order in a question.

    Why you can't drive?

4. Don't forget to use *do* or *does* with *have to* in questions.
    do
    Why ∧ you have to get a limited license?

EDITING QUIZ

Find the mistakes with the underlined words, and correct them. Not every sentence has a mistake. If the sentence is correct, write *C*.

does she have to
EXAMPLES: Why ~~she has to~~ take a driving class?

She can drive alone during the day. *C*

1. We have to coming to school for the class.

2. My brother should takes the vision test first.

3. The driving teacher can to explain the lesson very well.

4. What I have to do to get a permit?

5. He should studies the rules of the road.

6. Where can we practice?

7. What we should to learn for the written test?

8. Why older children have to use car seats?

1. What did you learn in this unit? Write three sentences in your notebook about each of these topics:
   - Driver's licenses
   - Gas stations
   - Children's car seats

2. Write three questions you still have about driving in the U.S.

EXPANSION ACTIVITIES

Writing Activity

In your notebook, write one negative and one affirmative sentence about each picture. Write about what is wrong with each picture.

EXAMPLE *This woman can't hold her baby in her arms in a car. The baby has to be in an infant seat.*

A. 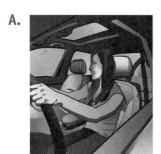   B.    C.

Outside Activity

Go to a local department store. Find a child's car seat and an infant seat. Tell the class how much they cost.

Internet Activity

Search the words *graduated licenses* and the name of your state. Find the rules for your state about limited licenses for teenagers.
   - What is the age for a full license?
   - How many young people can be in a car with a young driver?
   - When does a young driver have to be with an adult driver?
   - What hours can he/she drive?

UNIT

6

GRAMMAR
Must and *Have To*
Noncount Nouns
Quantity Expressions

CONTEXT
School

LESSON 1

GRAMMAR

Must
Must and *Have To*
Must Not and *Don't Have To*

CONTEXT

School Lunch Programs

Before You Read

1. Do elementary schools in your native country give free lunches to children?

2. What do children like to eat for lunch?

milk

vegetables/fruits   grains/bread   meats

SCHOOL LUNCH PROGRAMS

Children need good nutrition. The United States has a National School Lunch Program to give children balanced meals. Schools in this program **must** follow guidelines. They **must not** give children a lot of fat, sugar, or salt. They **must** serve food from each of these four groups:

- Meat
- Vegetables / fruits
- Grains / bread
- Milk

Children from very low-income families **don't have to** pay for a school lunch. Some families **have to** pay a small amount (less than 50¢). Some families have enough money and **have to** pay the full price. It isn't expensive. It's less than $2.00.

Parents **must** fill out an application for their children to get a free lunch. They **must** tell the truth about the family income.

Children **don't have to** eat the school lunch. They can bring a lunch from home. A popular lunch for children is a peanut butter and jelly sandwich.

Vocabulary
in Context

nutrition	Children need good **nutrition** to be healthy. They need to eat good food.
balanced	A **balanced** lunch contains items from each food group.
meal(s)	Breakfast, lunch, and dinner are **meals.**
serve	Schools give children lunch. They **serve** lunch every day.
guideline(s)	The National School Lunch Program makes **guidelines.** They tell the schools what to serve.
fat	Potato chips and French fries have a lot of **fat.**
grain(s)	We use **grains** to make bread and cereal.
income	They don't get much money at their job. They have a low **income.**
amount	Fifty cents is a small **amount** of money.
less than	The lunch costs $1.75. It's **less than** $2.00.
tell the truth	**Tell the truth** on the application. Don't give false information.

Did You Know?

The U.S. has food guidelines.

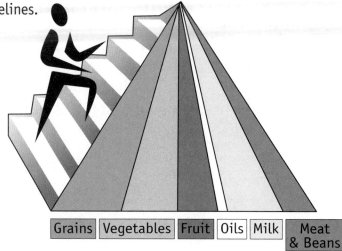

| Grains | Vegetables | Fruit | Oils | Milk | Meat & Beans |

 **Listening Activity**

Listen to the sentences about the reading. Circle *true* or *false*.

EXAMPLE (TRUE) FALSE

1. TRUE FALSE   5. TRUE FALSE
2. TRUE FALSE   6. TRUE FALSE
3. TRUE FALSE   7. TRUE FALSE
4. TRUE FALSE

6.1 | *Must*

Examples	Explanation
Schools **must** serve milk to children. Parents **must** fill out an application for the free lunch program.	We use *must* to show rules or laws.
School lunches **must not** have a lot of sugar. School lunches **must not** have a lot of fat.	When the rule is "don't do this," use *must not*.

EXERCISE 1 Fill in the blanks with one of the verbs from the box below. Use one verb twice.

| fill out | sign | pay ✓ | serve |

EXAMPLE The lunch is not free for everyone. Some families must ____*pay*____.

1. The school must _____ a nutritious lunch.

2. Parents must _____ an application for the school lunch program.

3. Parents must _____ the application.

4. Schools must _____ milk.

Bayside Public Schools
Application for Free and Reduced Price Meals

To apply for free and reduced price meals for your child(ren), you must fill out this form and sign it. You must tell the truth. Use a pen.

Part 1 List the names of children at school.

Name(s) of Child(ren) Last name, First name	Age	School	Grade	Class
1.				
2.				
3.				

Part 2 List the names of all household members and their monthly incomes.

Last name, First name	Monthly income
1.	
2.	
3.	

Part 3 Signature and Social Security Number

Signature of Household Member	Mailing Address
Social Security Number	Phone Number

			--			--					( )

For school use only

Date received _____ Date approved _____

EXERCISE **2** Look at the application for the school lunch program above. Change the sentences below from imperative statements to statements with *must*.

EXAMPLES Print your answers. You _____ *must print your answers.* _____

Don't use a pencil. You _____ *must not use a pencil.* _____

1. Fill out the application. You _____

2. Sign your name. You _____

3. Don't fill out the last box. You _____

4. Write your family income. You _____

5. Use a pen. You _____

6. Don't use a pencil. You _____

7. Don't give false information. You _____

6.2 | *Must* and *Have To*

Must and *have to* have very similar meanings.

Examples	Explanation
You **must** write your family income. You **have to** write your family income. Schools **must** serve children milk. Schools **have to** serve children milk.	*Must* is very formal. We use *must* for rules and laws. We can also use *have to* for rules and laws.
My daughter is hungry. I **have to** make lunch for her. It's late. We **have to** leave.	Use *have to* for personal necessity. Don't use *must* for personal necessity.

Language Note: In a question, *have to* is more common than *must*.
> Do I **have to** sign the application?
> Do schools **have to** serve children milk?

EXERCISE 3 Fill in the blanks with *must* + a verb to talk about rules.

EXAMPLE Students ___*must pay for*___ college courses.

1. When you see a red light, you _____.
2. On an application, you _____.
3. Drivers _____.
4. In a car, small children _____.
5. Immigrants _____.

EXERCISE 4 Fill in the blanks to talk about personal necessities. Answers will vary.

EXAMPLE I have to ___*call my mom*___ every day.

1. In class, we have to _____.
2. The teacher has to _____.
3. A mother has to _____.
4. Children have to _____.
5. College students have to _____.
6. I have to _____ every day.

6.3 | *Must Not* and *Don't Have To*

Have to and *must* have very similar meanings. *Don't have to* and *must not* have very different meanings.

Examples	Explanation
School lunches **must not** have a lot of fat. You must tell the truth. You **must not** give false information.	*Must not* gives a rule.
Children **don't have to** eat the school lunch. They can bring a lunch from home. Children of low income families **don't have to** pay for lunch. They can get a free lunch.	*Don't have to* shows that something is not necessary.

EXERCISE 5 ABOUT YOU Work with a partner. Name three things you *don't have to* do.

EXAMPLE I don't have to work on Saturdays.

EXERCISE 6 ABOUT YOU Work with a partner. Name three things students *must not do* at this school or in this class.

EXAMPLE Students must not talk in the library.

EXERCISE 7 Fill in the blanks with the negative of *must* or *have to*. Remember, they do NOT have the same meaning.

EXAMPLES Schools in the lunch program ___*must not*___ serve a lot of sugar.

Children ___*don't have to*___ be in the school lunch program.

1. Many families in the school lunch program _____ pay. Their children get free lunch.

2. Your son _____ eat at school. He can eat at home.

3. Parents _____ give false information on the application.

4. You _____ drink the milk. You can drink water.

5. We _____ study in the library. We can study at home.

6. You _____ talk loudly in the school library. It's a rule.

7. Children _____ come late to school.

LESSON 2

GRAMMAR

Count and Noncount Nouns
Quantity Expressions with Noncount Nouns
Much/A Lot of/A Little with Noncount Nouns
Some/Any with Noncount Nouns

CONTEXT

Maya's School Lunch

Before You Read

1. What foods are good for children?

2. What are some things children don't like to eat?

MAYA'S SCHOOL LUNCH

Victor: How are the lunches at your school? Do you like them?

Maya: Sometimes I do. Sometimes I don't. My favorite lunches are pizza, grilled cheese sandwiches, macaroni and cheese, and tacos. Sometimes we get **a piece of fish,** but I don't like fish.

Victor: What do you drink?

Maya: We always get **a small carton of milk.**

Victor: Do you get **any fruit?**

Maya: Yes. We always get a **piece of fruit**—an apple, an orange, a banana, or **a small bunch of grapes.** But the kids don't like the fruit. Sometimes we throw away the fruit.

Victor: That's terrible! Fruit is so good for you. Do the kids get **any soda?**

Maya: No. The teacher says that we shouldn't eat **much sugar.** But I love soda.

Victor: Your teacher's right. Sugar isn't good for you. Do all children get school lunches?

Maya: No. **Some kids** bring a lunch from home. My friend Wanda always brings her lunch to school in a lunch box. Her mother usually gives her a peanut butter and jelly sandwich and **a candy bar** or **a bag of potato chips.** She always brings **a small bottle of juice.** Juice is good for you, isn't it?

Victor: Juice contains **a lot of sugar.** Jelly contains **a lot of sugar** too. It's better to eat **a piece of fruit.** Please eat your fruit. Don't throw it away!

Maya: Dad, why do you always have **a can of soda** with you? It's better to drink **a bottle of water.**

Victor: You're right.

Vocabulary
in Context

favorite	I love pizza. Pizza is my **favorite** lunch.
bunch of	We get a small **bunch of** grapes with lunch.
throw away	Don't **throw away** the fruit. It's good for you.
terrible	It isn't good to throw away fruit. It's **terrible!**
lunch box	Some people take their lunches in a **lunch box.**
contain	Soda **contains** a lot of sugar.

Did You Know?

The national free lunch program provides free or low-cost lunches to 28 million children in the U.S.

 **Listening Activity**

Listen to the sentences about the conversation. Circle *true* or *false*.

EXAMPLE   TRUE   (FALSE)

1. TRUE   FALSE   5. TRUE   FALSE
2. TRUE   FALSE   6. TRUE   FALSE
3. TRUE   FALSE   7. TRUE   FALSE
4. TRUE   FALSE   8. TRUE   FALSE

6.4 | Count and Noncount Nouns

Examples	Explanation
I eat two **sandwiches** a day. Do you like **tacos?** Many **children** get a free lunch.	Some nouns are *count* nouns. We can count them. We can use a number with them. They have a singular and a plural form.
The school doesn't serve **candy.** **Pizza** is very popular. The school always serves **milk.** **Juice** contains a lot of **sugar.**	Some nouns are *noncount* nouns. We don't count them. We don't use a number with them. They have no plural form.

Common noncount nouns are:

milk	bread	pizza	meat	soup
butter	jelly	coffee	tea	juice
water	chicken	soda	fruit	cheese
cream	candy	corn	peanut butter	sugar
salt	pork	fat	macaroni	fish
oil	rice	popcorn		

EXERCISE 1 ABOUT YOU Tell how often you eat or drink each item. Practice noncount nouns (no plural form) and the frequency words from the box below.

always	every day	often	sometimes	rarely	never

EXAMPLES fruit
I eat fruit every day.

popcorn
I never eat popcorn.

coffee
I rarely drink coffee.

1. milk
2. tea
3. coffee
4. water
5. soda
6. juice
7. bread
8. rice

9. pizza
10. meat
11. chicken
12. fish
13. pork
14. popcorn
15. candy
16. jelly

EXERCISE 2 ABOUT YOU Tell how often you eat or drink each item. Practice using count nouns and the frequency words. You can use the singular or plural form.

EXAMPLES potato(es)
I eat potatoes at least once a week.

banana(s)
I eat one banana a day.

avocado(es)
I never eat avocadoes.

1. banana(s)
2. apple(s)
3. potato chip(s)
4. cookie(s)
5. grape(s)

6. egg(s)
7. cracker(s)
8. orange(s)
9. hamburger(s)
10. hot dog(s)

6.5 | Quantity Expressions with Noncount Nouns

Examples	Explanation
I eat **three pieces of fruit** a day. I drink **two cups of tea** a day. Children get **one carton of milk** with lunch.	To talk about quantity with a noncount noun, use a unit of measurement that you can count: *cup of, bowl of, carton of, teaspoon of, piece of*, etc.

Quantity Expressions with Noncount Nouns

a slice of pizza	a leaf of lettuce
a loaf of bread	a can of tuna
a slice of bread	an ear of corn
a piece of bread	a piece of fish
a slice of cheese	a piece of meat
a carton of milk	a piece of chicken
a gallon of milk	a jar of jelly
a glass of milk	a jar of peanut butter
a can of soda	a piece of candy
a cup of coffee	a piece of fruit
a pound of coffee	a teaspoon of salt
a cup of tea	a stick of butter
a glass of juice	a bowl of rice
a bottle of juice	a bowl of popcorn
a bottle of oil	a teaspoon of sugar
a bowl of soup	a jar of mayonnaise
a can of soup	a tablespoon of mayonnaise

EXERCISE 3 Complete this conversation with one of the words from the box below.

| can | jar | candy ✓ | fruit | milk |

Amy: Mom. I'm hungry. Can I have a piece of ___*candy*___?
                                                    (example)

Marta: You know it isn't good for you. Have a piece of _____.
                                                              (1)

Amy: Can I have a peanut butter and jelly sandwich, too? Where's the peanut butter?

Marta: You can find a _____ of peanut butter in the cabinet
                            (2)

next to the refrigerator.

Amy: I see a _____ of soda in the refrigerator. Can I have it too?
                    (3)

Marta: No. Soda has a lot of sugar. Drink a glass of _____.
                                                          (4)

EXERCISE 4 Victor is teaching Maya to make a tuna sandwich. Fill in the blanks with a quantity expression. Answers may vary.

Victor: You can find a fresh _____*loaf*_____ of bread on the table. Take
                                (example)

two _____ of bread and put them on a plate. Open a
      (1)

_____ of tuna and put the tuna in a bowl. You can find
   (2)

a _____ of mayonnaise in the refrigerator. Add two
    (3)

_____ of mayonnaise. Mix the tuna and mayonnaise.
   (4)

Put the tuna on the bread. Now you have a healthy lunch.

Maya: Dad, can I have a _____ of soda with my sandwich?
                              (5)

Victor: Sorry. But you can have a _____ of water with it. And
                                     (6)

you can have a _____ of fruit after lunch.
               (7)

EXERCISE 5 ABOUT YOU Add a quantity if possible.

EXAMPLE I eat _two slices_ of bread a day. OR _I don't eat bread_.

1. I drink _____ of water a day.

2. I eat _____ of fruit a day.

3. I put _____ of sugar in my coffee or tea.

4. I buy _____ of milk a week.

5. I drink _____ of tea a day.

6. I drink _____ of juice a week.

6.6 | *Much/A Lot of/A Little* with Noncount Nouns

Examples	Explanation
I eat **a lot of** cheese. I don't drink **a lot of** milk. I don't use **much** sugar.	Use *a lot of* with large quantities. In negatives, you can also use *much*.
He uses **a little** sugar. He drinks **a little** tea.	Use *a little* with small quantities.

Language Note: We say *use*, not *eat*, with **sugar, salt,** and **butter.** We add these things to food.

EXERCISE 6 ABOUT YOU Tell if you eat, drink, or use a lot of this item.

EXAMPLES milk
I don't drink a lot of milk.

meat
I eat a lot of meat.

salt
I don't use much salt.

1. cheese
2. popcorn
3. rice
4. candy
5. milk

6. coffee
7. salt
8. sugar
9. butter
10. soup

EXERCISE **7**   Fill in the blanks with *a little* and one of the words from the box below. Answers may vary.

meat	butter	milk	salt	sugar	oil✓

EXAMPLE   Use <u> *a little oil* </u> to cook.

1. Put _____ and _____ in the coffee.

2. The pizza has _____ and a lot of cheese.

3. Put _____ on the bread.

4. Put _____ in the soup.

6.7 | *Some/Any* with Noncount Nouns

Examples	Explanation
A: Does the pizza have **any** meat? B: Yes. The pizza has **some** meat. A: Do kids get **any** soda with their lunches? B: No. They don't get **any** soda. A: Do you want **some** coffee? B: No. I don't want **any** coffee.	We use *any* or *some* in questions. We use *some* in affirmatives. We use *any* in negatives.

EXERCISE **8**   Fill in the blanks with *some* or *any*.

EXAMPLE   The pizza has _____*some*_____ meat.

1. I don't want _____ soda.

2. The school lunch doesn't have _____ candy.

3. Do you want _____ milk?

4. No. I don't want _____ milk.

5. The sandwich has _____ mayonnaise.

6. Does the soup have _____ salt?

7. She's a vegetarian. She doesn't eat _____ meat.

8. I can't buy my lunch today. I don't have _____ money.

9. You should eat _____ fruit every day.

GRAMMAR

Count and Noncount Nouns with *Some/Any*
Count vs. Noncount Nouns: *A Lot of/Much/Many*
Count vs. Noncount Nouns: *A Few/A Little*
Count vs. Noncount Nouns: *How Much/How Many*

CONTEXT

School Supplies

Before You Read

1. What do children need for school?

2. Should children have a lot of homework?

SCHOOL SUPPLIES

It is September. It's the first day of school. Victor's daughter, Maya, has a list of information about school and school supplies.

Victor: What's this?

Maya: It's a note from school. It has **a lot of information** about the school. And this is my list of school supplies. I need **a lot of supplies** for school.

Victor: **How many things** do you need?

Maya: I need **two erasers, one ruler, two spiral notebooks, ten pencils, one glue stick, one pair of scissors, one large package of notebook paper, four folders, one box of tissues, and one box of crayons.**

Victor: **How many crayons** are in one box?

Maya: You can buy a box of 8, 16, 24, 36, or 48. We need at least 24.

Victor calls Simon for help.

Victor: I have **a few questions** about my daughter's school. Do you have **any time** now?

Simon: Yes, Victor. I have **a little free time** now.

Victor: My daughter has a list of school supplies. Where do I buy them?

Simon: **Many stores** sell school supplies, but the office supply store near my house has a sale on school supplies now. I have **a few coupons.** We can go together.

Victor: Do I have to buy **any books? How much money** do I need for books?

Simon: You don't have to buy **any books** for public school. The school gives books to the students.

Victor: That's good. The note from school has **a lot of information** about homework. Do American kids get **a lot of homework?**

Simon: Yes, they do.

Victor: One more question. Do I have to buy a uniform for my daughter?

Simon: I don't know. Children in some schools need uniforms. Read me the information from your daughter's school.

Victor: OK.

Vocabulary in Context

note	The teacher sometimes writes a **note** to parents.
information	I need **information** about the program.
school supplies	Children need **school supplies**, like pencils and paper.
coupon	Here's a **coupon.** You can get two notebooks for the price of one with this coupon.
uniform	In some schools, all the children wear the same **uniform.**

Did You Know?

- The average class in an American elementary school has 25 students.
- Most students are five years old when they start school.

Listening Activity   Listen to the sentences about the conversation. Circle *true* or *false*.

EXAMPLE   (TRUE)   FALSE

1. TRUE   FALSE   5. TRUE   FALSE

2. TRUE   FALSE   6. TRUE   FALSE

3. TRUE   FALSE   7. TRUE   FALSE

4. TRUE   FALSE

6.8 | Count and Noncount Nouns with *Some/Any*

Examples	Explanation
Maya has **some** information from her teacher. Victor has **some** questions.	Use *some* with noncount nouns and plural count nouns.
Does she need **any/some** glue? Does she need **any/some** pencils?	Use *any* or *some* with both noncount nouns and plural count nouns in questions.
She doesn't have **any** homework. She doesn't have **any** folders.	Use *any* with both noncount nouns and plural count nouns in negatives.

Language Note: *Homework* and *information* are noncount nouns. They have no plural form. To add a specific quantity, we can say *a homework assignment* and *a piece of information*.

EXERCISE ▮1▮   Fill in the blanks with *some* or *any*.

EXAMPLE   I need ___*some*___ paper for school.

1. Do you have _____ homework today?

2. They have _____ math homework.

3. I don't have _____ problems with my homework.

4. He needs _____ school supplies.

5. I don't need _____ paper for my gym class.

6. Do you need _____ erasers for school?

7. We need _____ crayons for school.

EXERCISE 2 ABOUT YOU Answer the questions. Use *some* or *any* in your answers.

EXAMPLE Do you have any time to watch TV?
Yes. I have some time to watch TV after school.

1. Do you have any homework today?

2. Do you need any books for this course?

3. Does this class have any students from Korea?

4. Do you need any paper to do this exercise?

5. Do you have any information about universities in the U.S.?

6.9 | Count vs. Noncount Nouns: *A Lot Of/Much/Many*

	Examples	Explanation
Count	Maya needs **a lot of/many** school supplies. Does she need **a lot of/many** crayons? She doesn't need **a lot of/many** notebooks.	Use *a lot of* or *many* with count nouns.
Noncount	Does Victor have **a lot of/much** information about the school? He doesn't have **a lot of/much** money. Maya needs **a lot of** paper.	Use *a lot of* or *much* with noncount nouns in questions and negatives. In affirmative statements, use *a lot of*, not *much*.

EXERCISE 3 Circle the correct answer. In some cases, both answers are possible.

EXAMPLE I have (*much* /(*a lot of*)) paper, but I don't have ((*many*)/ *much*) pencils.

1. Some children drink (*much* / *a lot of*) soda, but they don't drink (*many* / *much*) water.

2. I eat (*a lot of* / *many*) fruit, but I don't eat (*much* / *many*) bananas.

3. (*Many* / *Much*) stores have school supply sales in August.

4. I need (*a lot of* / *much*) information about schools in the U.S.

5. Children need (*a lot of* / *much*) school supplies.

6. I have (*much* / *a lot of*) homework, but I don't have (*much* / *many*) time to do it.

7. (*Many* / *A lot of*) children get a free lunch in the U.S.

6.10 | Count vs. Noncount Nouns: *A Few/A Little*

	Examples	Explanation
Count	Maya needs **a few** erasers. She needs **a few** pencils.	Use *a few* with count nouns.
Noncount	Dorota has **a little** time on Saturday. School lunches cost **a little** money.	Use *a little* with noncount nouns.

EXERCISE **4**   Fill in the blanks with *a few* or *a little*.

EXAMPLE   Maya drinks ___*a little*___ juice every day.

1. Victor has _____ time to help Maya with her homework.

2. Maya has _____ good friends at school.

3. Maya watches _____ TV programs after dinner.

4. She has _____ time to watch TV every day.

5. She needs _____ pencils for school.

EXERCISE **5**   ABOUT YOU Fill in the blanks.

EXAMPLE   I have a few *good friends* .

1. I need a little _____ .

2. I know a few _____ .

3. I eat a little _____ every day.

4. I eat a few _____ every week.

5. I use a little _____ .

6.11 | Count vs. Noncount Nouns: *How Much/How Many*

Examples	Explanation
How many coupons do you have? **How many** crayons do you need for school?	Use *how many* with count nouns.
How much paper does she need? **How much** money do I need for books?	Use *how much* with noncount nouns.
How much does this book cost? **How much** is the school lunch?	Use *how much* to ask about cost.

EXERCISE **6**   ABOUT YOU Find a partner. Ask these questions about an elementary school in your partner's native country.

EXAMPLE   How many days a week do kids go to school?
They go to school five days a week.

1. How many months a year do kids go to school?

2. How many kids are in an average class?

3. How much time do kids spend on homework?

4. How many hours a day are kids in school?

5. How much time do kids have for vacation?

6. How much money do kids spend on books?

7. Do kids get school lunch? How much does it cost?

8. Do kids wear a uniform? How much does a uniform cost?

EXERCISE **7**   ABOUT YOU Fill in the blanks with *much* or *many*.

EXAMPLE   How ____*many*____ lessons do we do a day?

1. How _____ classes do you have now?

2. How _____ money do you need to take one cless?

3. How _____ paper do you need for your homework?

4. How _____ students in this class speak Spanish?

5. How _____ books do you need for this course?

6. How _____ time do you need for homework?

7. How _____ homework do you have with you today?

8. How _____ dictionaries do you have?

EXERCISE **8** *Combination Exercise.* Circle the correct word in parentheses ( ) to complete this conversation between Victor and his neighbor, Marco. Sometimes more than one answer is possible.

Marco: I have (*a little* / *a few*) questions. I need (*a little* / *a few*)
(example)   (1)

information. Do you have (*any* / *some*) time to answer my
(2)

questions?

Victor: Yes. I have (*a little* / *a few*) time right now.
(3)

Marco: Can my kids get into the free lunch program?

Victor: Maybe. If you don't earn (*many* / *much*) money, they can
(4)

probably get into the free lunch program.

Marco: I don't earn (*many* / *a lot of*) money. What should I do?
(5)

Victor: You have to fill out a form. The form has (*many* / *much*) questions.
(6)

Marco: How (*much* / *many*) does a school lunch cost?
(7)

Victor: The full price is $1.75. That's not (*much* / *any*) money.
(8)

Marco: I have (*a lot of* / *much*) kids in school, so for me it's (*much* / *a lot of*)
(9)   (10)

money.

Victor: How (*much* / *many*) kids do you have?
(11)

Marco: Six. Four are in school, so I really need to learn about the free lunch program.

EDITING ADVICE

1. Don't put *a* or *an* before a noncount noun.

   I like to eat a rice.

2. Use *of* with a unit of measure.

               of
   I want a cup‿coffee.

3. Don't forget *of* with *a lot of*.

               of
   I don't have a lot‿homework today.

4. Don't confuse *much* and *many, a little* and *a few.*

           many
   He doesn't have ~~much~~ friends.

        few
   I eat a ~~little~~ grapes every day.

        little
   Put a ~~few~~ salt in the soup.

5. Don't use *much* in affirmative statements.

          a lot of
   He drinks ~~much~~ soda.

EDITING QUIZ

Find the mistakes with the underlined words, and correct them. Not every sentence has a mistake. If the sentence is correct, write *C*.

EXAMPLES   *of*
Do you drink a lot‿milk?

I drink a little milk every day.   *C*

1. I eat <u>an</u> apple every day. I don't eat <u>a</u> bread every day.

2. Do you want a <u>can</u> soda?

3. We have to read <u>a little</u> pages every day.

4. Please put <u>a few</u> sugar in my coffee.

5. I don't like to eat <u>a</u> grapes.

6. Children need <u>a lot</u> school supplies.

7. How <u>much</u> cups of coffee do you drink a day?

8. I have <u>a little</u> time to help you on Saturday.

1. What did you learn in this unit? Write three sentences in your note-book about each of these topics:
   - Government rules for school lunch programs
   - Foods in school lunch programs
   - Healthy foods
   - School supplies

2. Write three questions you still have about American elementary schools.

EXPANSION ACTIVITIES

Writing Activities

1. In your notebook, rewrite the following paragraph. Change the underlined food to a specific amount of the food. Use the quantity expressions you learned in this unit.

   I try to eat for good health every day. For example, I drink <u>water</u> before each meal. Then, I'm not so hungry. I don't have <u>soda</u> with every meal. I drink <u>tea</u> and not coffee after a meal. I have <u>cereal</u> for breakfast. I have salad with <u>soup</u> for lunch. In cold weather, I like <u>meat</u> for lunch. I eat <u>fruit</u> every day too. And, I try to eat <u>fish</u> once a week.

   EXAMPLE *I drink a glass of water before each meal.*

2. Use information from Exercise 6 on page 131 to write a short paragraph of five or six sentences about schools in your partner's country.

Outside Activity

Ask an elementary school child about his/her school. Tell the class the name of the child's school and some interesting facts about this child's school. What does the child like about the school?

Internet Activities

1. Go to the government's Web site on school lunches (www.fns.usda.gov/cnd/Lunch/default.htm). Click on "Program Fact Sheet." Find a few interesting facts about the program. (You can also search the name of your state with the words "school lunch program" for information in your state.)

2. Search the words *fat counter* on a search engine. Find a list of foods showing fat and sodium (salt) content. How much fat is in *one* of your meals today? How much salt?

GRAMMAR
Prepositions
There Is/There Are

CONTEXT
Shopping

LESSON

GRAMMAR

Prepositions of Time
Time Expressions Without Prepositions
Prepositions of Place
Prepositions in Common Expressions

CONTEXT

Twenty-Four/Seven

Before You Read

1. Do you ever shop late at night? Why or why not?
2. Do you ever shop at a convenience store? Why or why not?

TWENTY-FOUR/SEVEN

Sue: Look. We're out of coffee. We need coffee for tomorrow morning. Can you go out and buy some?

Rick: Now? It's late. It's **after 9:30.** We can get it **in the morning.**

Sue: Tomorrow is Saturday. The stores are crowded **on Saturday.** I don't like to shop **on the weekend.** Anyway, we like to drink coffee **in the morning.**

Rick: But the supermarket is closed **at night.**

Sue: You're right. But the convenience store is open. It's open 24/7.

Rick: My news program is on TV **at 10 p.m.** I don't have time **before** the news program. It starts **in 20 minutes.**

Sue: You can go **after the news.**

(*Rick is now **at** the convenience store. Sue calls him **on** his cell phone.*)

Rick: Hello?

Sue: Hi. Are you **at** the convenience store now?

Rick: I'm still **in** the car. I'm **in** the parking lot.

Sue: Can you go **to** the pharmacy too and get some aspirin? I have a headache.

Rick: Can I get the aspirin **at** the convenience store?

Sue: You can, but aspirin is on sale this week **at** the pharmacy—two bottles for $5.00.

Rick: Where's the pharmacy?

Sue: It's **near** the convenience store. It's **on** the corner. It's **next to** the gas station.

Rick: Is the pharmacy open too?

Sue: Yes, it's open 24/7.

Rick: Does anyone sleep at night?

Vocabulary
in Context

out of	We don't have any coffee. We're **out of** coffee.
convenience store	A **convenience store** is open late. It's a small supermarket.
24/7	**24/7** means a place is open 24 hours a day, seven days a week.
pharmacy	You can buy medicine in a **pharmacy.**
aspirin / headache	Take an **aspirin** for your **headache.**
corner	The store is on the **corner** of Main Street and Willow Street.

- When you see a sign *Two for $5.00,* you usually don't need to buy two. You can buy one for $2.50.
- Prices at a convenience store are sometimes high. You are paying for the convenience of 24/7.

Listening Activity

Listen to the sentences about the conversation. Circle *true* or *false.*

EXAMPLE (TRUE)   FALSE

1. TRUE	FALSE		5. TRUE	FALSE
2. TRUE	FALSE		6. TRUE	FALSE
3. TRUE	FALSE		7. TRUE	FALSE
4. TRUE	FALSE			

7.1 | Prepositions of Time

Prepositions are connecting words. We can use prepositions with time expressions.		
The store is open	**in** the morning.	
	in the afternoon.	
	in the evening.	
	at night.	
The news program starts	**at** 10 p.m.	
	in 20 minutes.	
You can go out	**after** 9:30.	
	after the news program.	
	after work.	
Sue goes to sleep	**before** 10:30.	
The stores are crowded	**on** Saturdays.	
	on the weekend.	

Language Note: A sentence can have two time expressions.

I go to work **at** 7 o'clock **in** the morning.

I wake up **at** 9 a.m. **on** the weekend.

EXERCISE 1 Fill in the blanks with the correct preposition of time: *in, on, after,* or *at.*

EXAMPLE Sue and Rick don't work ____at____ night.

1. They work _____ Monday.

2. They don't work _____ the evening.

3. The convenience store is open _____ night.

4. They don't work _____ the weekend.

5. They can buy milk _____ the morning.

6. Many stores open _____ 9 a.m.

7. It's 9:37 now. It's _____ 9:30 p.m.

8. We go shopping _____ the afternoon.

EXERCISE 2 ABOUT YOU Ask a question with *When do you . . .* and the words given. Another student will answer.

EXAMPLES watch TV

A: When do you watch TV?
B: I watch TV at night.

1. drink coffee
2. watch the news on TV
3. go to sleep
4. wake up
5. go shopping

6. take a shower
7. eat lunch
8. read the newspaper
9. see your friends
10. do your homework

7.2 | Time Expressions Without Prepositions

In some cases, we don't use a preposition with time.	
The store is open	**24 hours a day.**
The store is open	**seven days a week.**
We shop	**three times a month.**
They buy milk	**once a week.**
We cook	**twice a day.**
The convenience store is open	**24/7.**
The convenience store is open	**all day and all night.**

EXERCISE **3**   Fill in the blanks with one of the expressions of time without a preposition. (See 7.2 on page 139).

EXAMPLE   The pharmacy near Rick's house is open _____*24 hours a day*_____.

1. Rick watches the news _____.

2. Most supermarkets in this city are open _____.

3. Most banks in this city are open _____.

4. Most people in my country shop for food _____.

EXERCISE **4**   ABOUT YOU Ask a question with *how many* and the words given. Another student will answer.

EXAMPLE   days a week / work

A: How many days a week do you work?
B: I work five days a week.

1. times a day / check your e-mail
2. hours a day / talk on the phone
3. times a month / go to the library
4. times a day / brush your teeth

5. hours a night / sleep
6. times a day / cook
7. hours a day / watch TV
8. times a week / shop for food

7.3 | Prepositions of Place

We can use prepositions with locations.

Preposition	Examples
in	Rick is **in** the car. He is **in** the parking lot.
near	The pharmacy is **near** the convenience store.
next to	The pharmacy is **next to** the gas station.
on	The convenience store is **on** the corner.
at	Rick is **at** the convenience store. Sue is **at** home. You are **at** school. My parents are **at** work.
to	Go **to** the pharmacy.

Language Note: COMPARE:

I'm **in** the store. (I'm not outside the store.)
I'm **at** the store. (I may be inside or in the parking lot, ready to go in.)

EXERCISE 5 This is a phone conversation between Victor and Lisa. Lisa is at home. Victor is on his cell phone in his car. Fill in the blanks with the correct preposition: *in*, *on*, *at*, *near*, or *next to*.

Victor: Hello?

Lisa: Hi. It's Lisa. Where are you now?

Victor: I'm ___*at*___ school. Where are you?
(example)

Lisa: I'm _____ home. Are you _____ class?
(1)   (2)

Victor: No, I'm _____ the parking lot. My class starts in ten minutes.
(3)

Lisa: Can you go _____ the store on your way home?
(4)

We need milk. There's a sale on milk _____ Tom's Market.

Victor: Where's Tom's Market?

Lisa: It's _____ the school. It's _____ the corner.
(6)   (7)

It's _____ the Laundromat.
(8)

7.4 | Prepositions in Common Expressions

We can use prepositions in many common expressions.	
on	Rick is **on the phone.**
	The news program is **on TV.** You can hear the news **on the radio.**
	Aspirin is **on sale.**
for	Aspirin is on sale this week, two bottles **for** $5.00.
in	The coffee is **in** aisle three.
of	We don't have any coffee. We're out **of** coffee.

EXERCISE **6** This is a conversation between Simon and Marta. Fill in the blanks with *on*, *in*, *next to*, *of*, *after*, or *for*.

Simon: I'm going to the store ___*after*___ work. Eggs are on
(example)

sale—two dozen _____ $1.89.
(1)

Marta: Buy mangoes, too. They're _____ sale—three
(2)

_____ $1.49.
(3)

Simon: Anything else?

Marta: Oh, yes. Buy coffee, too.

Simon: Are we out _____ coffee? So soon?
(4)

Marta: Yes. We drink a lot of coffee.

Simon: Anything else?

Marta: No. Come home right away. Your favorite show is

_____ TV at 7 p.m.
(5)

(*Simon is at the store now. He asks a store clerk for information.*)

Simon: Where's the coffee?

Clerk: It's _____ aisle four.
(6)

Simon: I don't see it. Can you help me find it?

Clerk: Sure. Here it is. It's _____ the tea.
(7)

EXERCISE 7 *Combination Exercise.* This is a conversation between Rick and Sue. Fill in the blanks with the correct preposition: *in, on, at, to,* or *after.*

Sue: Hi. I'm _____on_____ my cell phone.
(example)

Rick: Are you _____ the car?
(1)

Sue: No, I'm still _____ work. I can't come home right now.
(2)

_____ work, I have to make a few stops. I can be home
(3)

_____ about an hour and a half.
(4)

Rick: Where do you need to go?

Sue: I need to buy gas. Then I have to go _____ the dry cleaner.
(5)

Rick: Then can you come home?

Sue: No. Then I have to go to the post office. The post office closes
_____ 6 p.m.
(6)

Rick: Why do you have to do all of this now? Tomorrow is Saturday. We
can do these things tomorrow.

Sue: I don't like to do these things _____ Saturday. These
(7)

places are crowded _____ the weekend.
(8)

Rick: But I have dinner _____ the table now. Don't be too late.
(9)

LESSON 2

GRAMMAR

There Is and *There Are*
Negative Forms with *There Is/There Are*
Quantity Words

CONTEXT

Good Prices or Good Service

Before You Read

1. Which is better—good service or good prices?

2. Do you prefer big stores or small stores?

GOOD PRICES OR GOOD SERVICE

Conversation 1—In a big store

Rick: We need lightbulbs. **There's** a coupon in the newspaper for lightbulbs. Let's go to the home supply store.

Sue: (*At the store*) **There are** so many things in this store. How can we find what we need?

Rick: **There's** a clerk over there in the lighting department. Let's ask him. Excuse me, sir. I need to find lightbulbs. **There are** lamps here, but **there are no** lightbulbs.

Clerk: Lightbulbs are in aisle three. **There's** a clerk in aisle three.

Sue: (*After visiting aisle three*) I can't find the lightbulbs. And **there's no** clerk in aisle three. Can you help us?

Clerk: Sorry. That's not my department.

Sue: (*To Rick*) **There aren't** enough clerks in this store. **There isn't** good service in this store.

Rick: But I like this store. **There are** good prices here.

Conversation 2—In a small store

Clerk: Can I help you?

Peter: Yes. I need lightbulbs.

Clerk: Lightbulbs are downstairs, but **there isn't an** elevator in the store. I can get the lightbulbs for you.

Peter: Thanks for your help. (*Thinking*) I like this store. **There's** good service here. **There are** helpful clerks here. I prefer a small store with good service.

Vocabulary
in Context

service	Peter likes good **service**. He likes help in a store.
lightbulb	Rick needs a **lightbulb** for his lamp.
home supply store	A **home supply store** has many things for the home: tools, lightbulbs, paint, etc.
clerk	A **clerk** works to help people in a store.
lamp	The **lamp** is in the living room.
enough	There are a lot of shoppers, but there aren't **enough** clerks.
downstairs	We're on the first floor. Lightbulbs are **downstairs.**
elevator	Peter needs an **elevator** to go downstairs.
prefer	Peter **prefers** a store with good service.

Some people prefer small stores because they know the owners and get personal service. Some people prefer big stores because they have a lot of items and the prices are often lower.

Listening Activity   Listen to the sentences about the picture and story. Circle *true* or *false*.

EXAMPLE   (TRUE)   FALSE

1. TRUE   FALSE   4. TRUE   FALSE

2. TRUE   FALSE   5. TRUE   FALSE

3. TRUE   FALSE

7.5 | *There Is* and *There Are*

Singular

There	*is*	*a/an/one*	Singular Subject	Prepositional Phrase
There	is	a	coupon	in the newspaper.
There	is	an	elevator	in the store.
There	is	one	clerk	in the lighting department.

Language Note: The contraction for *there is* = *there's*.

Plural

There	*are*	Plural Word	Plural Subject	Prepositional Phrase
There	are		good prices	in the big store.
There	are	five	clerks	in the store.
There	are	a lot of	items	in the big store.

Language Note: *There are* has no contraction.

EXERCISE 1 Fill in the blanks with *there is* or *there are*. Use contractions where possible.

EXAMPLE _____*There are*_____ a lot of items in the big store.

1. _____ a sale on lightbulbs this week.

2. _____ lightbulbs in aisle three.

3. _____ a helpful clerk in the small store.

4. _____ many shoppers in the big store.

5. _____ a sign near the lightbulbs.

EXERCISE 2 This is a cell phone conversation between Simon and Victor. Fill in the blanks with *there is* or *there are*. Make a contraction whenever possible.

Simon: Hello?

Victor: Hi, Simon. It's Victor.

Simon: Are you at home?

Victor: No, I'm not. I'm at the department store with my wife. ___*There's*___
(example)

a big sale at this store—50% off all winter items. Lisa loves sales.

She wants to buy a winter coat. _____ a
(1)

lot of women in the coat department, but _____ only one
(2)

clerk. Where are you?

Simon: I'm at home. _____ a football game on TV.
(3)

Victor: I know. I think all the men are at home in front of the TV.

_____ only one man in the department—me.
(4)

Simon: That's too bad. It's a great game.

Victor: It's not so bad. _____ a TV in the store, and _____ a
(5)   (6)

nice sofa in front of the TV. So I can watch while my wife shops.

Simon: I prefer to watch the game at home with my friends.

Victor: Me too.

7.6 | Negative Forms with *There Is/There Are*

We can use *there isn't/there aren't* for the negative.

Negative Singular

There	isn't	a/an	Singular Subject	Prepositional Phrase
There	**isn't**	a	clerk	in aisle three.
There	**isn't**	an	elevator	in the big store.
There's		*no*	Singular Subject	Prepositional Phrase
There's		no	clerk	in aisle three.
There's		no	elevator	in the big store.

Negative Plural

There	aren't	any	Plural Subject	Prepositional Phrase
There	**aren't**	any	lightbulbs	in this aisle.
There	**aren't**	any	helpful clerks	in the big store.
There	*are*	*no*	Plural Subject	Prepositional Phrase
There	**are**	no	lightbulbs	in this aisle.
There	**are**	no	helpful clerks	in this store.

EXERCISE 3 Change to a negative statement.

EXAMPLE There's a small hardware store near my house. _____There isn't_____ a big store near my house.

1. There are 20 aisles in the big store. _____ 20 aisles in the small store.

2. There are lightbulbs in aisle three. _____ any lightbulbs in aisle five.

3. There's usually a clerk in aisle three. _____ a clerk in aisle three now.

4. There's an elevator in the small store. _____ an elevator in the big store.

5. There's good service in the small store. _____ good service in the big store.

7.7 | Quantity Words

Quantity	Examples
xxxxxx	There are **many/a lot of** lightbulbs in the store.
xxx	There are **some** lamps in aisle three.
xx	There aren't **enough** clerks in the big store.
x	There is **one/an** elevator in the small store.
0	There aren't **any** lightbulbs in aisle three. There are **no** lightbulbs in aisle three.

EXERCISE 4 ABOUT YOU Use *there is/there are* and the words given to tell about your class and your school. Use quantity words from the chart above.

EXAMPLES teacher
There's one teacher in this class.

Korean student(s)
There are some Korean students in this class.

1. desk for all students
2. elevator(s)
3. computer(s)

4. young student(s)
5. telephone(s)
6. African student(s)

EXERCISE 5 ABOUT YOU Fill in the blanks to tell about the place where you live.

EXAMPLE There are no _____*old people*_____ in my building.

1. There's no _____ in my building.

2. There aren't many _____ in my building.

3. There are a lot of _____ in my building.

4. There are some _____ in my apartment.

5. There aren't enough _____ in my apartment.

6. There's a(n) _____ in my kitchen.

7. There aren't any _____ in my bedroom.

EXERCISE 6   This is a conversation between Rick and Sue. Fill in the blanks with *any, some, many, a lot of, enough, one, a,* or *no* to complete this conversation. In some cases, more than one answer is possible.

Sue: Where are the batteries? I need _____*some*_____ batteries for the
                                          (example)

      flashlight.

Rick: Look in the hall closet.

Sue: There aren't _____ batteries in the closet.
                         (1)

Rick: Look in the kitchen. There are _____ batteries there, I think.
                                         (2)

Sue: There's only _____ battery here. This flashlight needs two
                           (3)

      batteries. We need to go to the hardware store and get more

      batteries.

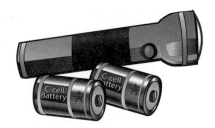

Rick: Let's go to the big store.

Sue: I prefer the small store. There's _____ service in a big store.
                                          (4)

      There aren't _____ clerks to help you. You have questions,
                         (5)

      but there are _____ clerks to answer your questions.
                     (6)

Rick: I don't have _____ questions about batteries. A battery is a
                        (7)

      battery. Look at this section of the newspaper. There are

      _____ things on sale at the big store—hundreds of things.
         (8)

Sue: We don't need hundreds of things. We just need batteries.

EXERCISE 7 This is a conversation between Rick and Sue. Fill in the blanks with the missing words from the box below. You can combine two words to fill in one blank. Make a contraction wherever possible.

there	they	is	are
it	no	isn't	aren't

Rick: Let's go to the hardware store today. ___*There's*___ a sale on
(example)

tools. _____ really cheap today.
(1)

Sue: Let's go to the department store. _____ a sale on all
(2)

shoes. _____ 50 percent off. Let's go to the department store
(3)

first and then to the hardware store.

Rick: _____ enough time. It's almost 4:00. The hardware
(4)

store closes at 5:30. _____ Saturday today, and the
(5)

hardware store _____ open late on Saturday.
(6)

Sue: The small hardware store _____ open late, but the big
(7)

store is open 24/7. You know, I don't really want to go to the

hardware store with you. Tools don't interest me. I have an idea.

You can go to the hardware store, and I can go to the department

store. I need shoes.

Rick: Need or want? You have 20 pairs of shoes.

Sue: _____ all old. I need new shoes.
(8)

Rick: And I need new tools.

LESSON 3

GRAMMAR

Yes/No Questions with *There Is/There Are*
Information Questions with *There Is/There Are*

CONTEXT

Choices

1. Is it easy to make choices in a store? Why or why not?
2. Some items, such as shampoo, are cheap and some are expensive. Is there a difference between cheap and expensive brands?

CHOICES

Halina and Peter are in the supermarket.

Peter: There are a lot of shampoos. **Why are there** so many shampoos? Do people need so many choices?

Halina: I don't think so. **Is there** any difference between this shampoo for $2.99 and that shampoo for $7.99?

Peter: I don't know. Let's buy the cheaper one.

Halina: OK. There's probably no difference.

Peter: **Are there** any other items on the shopping list?

Halina: Just two. We need sugar. The sugar is in aisle 6.

(in aisle 6)

Halina: This bag says 25 ounces for 89¢. That one says five pounds for $2.59. Which one is a better buy?

Peter: I don't know. What's an ounce?

Halina: It's part of a pound.

Peter: **How many ounces are there** in a pound?

Halina: Sixteen.

Peter: We need a calculator.

Halina: No, we don't. Look. There's a small sign under the sugar. The five-pound bag is about 2.9¢ an ounce. The 25-ounce bag is about 3.5¢ an ounce. The big bag is cheaper.

Peter: You're a smart shopper. Are we finished? **Is there** anything else on the list?

Halina: Yes. There's one more thing—dog food.

Peter: Wow! Look. There are over 20 kinds of dog food.

Halina: Dogs have choices too.

Vocabulary in Context

shampoo	I need to wash my hair. I need **shampoo.**
choice(s)	There are 50 shampoos. There are a lot of **choices.**
difference between	What's the **difference between** this shampoo and that one?
better buy	The large bag of sugar is a **better buy.** We can save money.
calculator	I need a **calculator** to do math.
about	This bag is 2.9¢ an ounce. It's **about** 3¢ an ounce.

- One pound = .45 kilograms
- One ounce = 28.35 grams

🎧 Listening Activity

Listen to the sentences about the conversation. Circle *true* or *false*.

EXAMPLE ⬭TRUE⬭   FALSE

1. TRUE   FALSE   4. TRUE   FALSE
2. TRUE   FALSE   5. TRUE   FALSE
3. TRUE   FALSE   6. TRUE   FALSE

7.8 | Yes/No Questions with *There Is/There Are*

Statement	Question	Short Answer
There's an aisle of shampoo.	**Is there** an aisle of tools in this store?	No, there isn't.
There are large bags of sugar.	**Are there** any small bags of sugar?	Yes, there are.
There's dog food in this aisle.	**Is there** any cat food in this aisle?	Yes, there is.

Language Notes:
1. We often add *any* to a question with noncount and plural count nouns.
2. Don't make a contraction in a singular short answer.
     Yes, ~~there's.~~   Yes. There is.

EXERCISE 1   Finish the short answers.

EXAMPLE   Are there any clerks in the store? Yes, _____*there are*_____.

1. Is there a price on the shampoo bottles? No, _____.

2. Are there a lot of shoppers in the store? Yes, _____.

3. Is there any dog food on sale this week? Yes, _____.

4. Are there a lot of choices of dog food? No, _____.

5. Is there a price under the bags of sugar? Yes, _____.

EXERCISE 2 Finish the question.

EXAMPLE <u>Is there</u> good service in a small store? Yes, there is.

1. _____ any shoppers in the dog food aisle?
   Yes, there are.

2. _____ a clerk in the dog food aisle? No, there isn't.

3. _____ a good price on shampoo this week?
   No, there isn't.

4. _____ any coupons for shampoo in the newspaper?
   Yes, there are.

5. _____ an elevator in the supermarket? No, there isn't.

6. _____ a lot of shoppers today?

EXERCISE 3 ABOUT YOU Ask a question with *is there* or *are there any* and the words given. Another student will answer.

EXAMPLE an elevator / in this building

A: Is there an elevator in this building?
B: No, there isn't.

1. Mexican students / in this class

2. hard exercises / in this lesson

3. new words / in this lesson

4. a verb chart / in your dictionary

5. a computer lab / at this school

6. public telephones / on this floor

7. a gym / at this school

7.9 | Information Questions with *There Is/There Are*

How much/how many, what else, and *why* are common question words with *is there/are there.* Notice question word order.

Question Word	is/are	there	Phrase	Answer
How much sugar	**is**	**there**	in the bag?	One pound.
How many ounces	**are**	**there**	in a pound?	16
What else	**is**	**there**	on the list?	Just one more thing.
Why	**are**	**there**	20 different kinds of shampoo?	I don't know.

Compare *yes/no* questions and information questions.

Yes/No Questions	Information Questions
Are there ten things on the list?	How many things **are there** on the list?
Are there different kinds of shampoo?	Why **are there** different kinds of shampoo?
Are there many kinds of dog food?	How many kinds of dog food **are there**?
Is there a difference between this shampoo and that shampoo?	Why **is there** a difference in price?

EXERCISE 4   Read the statements. Write an information question with the words in parentheses ( ).

EXAMPLE   There are ten kinds of dog food. (how many / shampoo)
How many kinds of shampoo are there?

1. There is one more thing on the list. (what else)

   _____

2. There are 16 ounces in a pound. (how many / in two pounds)

   _____

3. There are people in this line. (how many)

   _____

4. There are many kinds of dog food. (why)

   _____

5. There is a pharmacy in the store. (what else)

_____

6. There's money in my pocket. (how much)

_____

EXERCISE 5 ABOUT YOU Use the following words to ask and answer questions about your class or school. Follow the examples.

EXAMPLES desks / in this class

    A: How many desks are there in this class?
    B: There are 20 desks in this class.

1. students / in this class

2. windows / in this room

3. paper / on the floor

4. telephones / in this room

5. men's washrooms / on this floor

6. floors / in this building

7. pages / in this book

8. grammar information / on this page

EXERCISE 6 Write questions and answers for the items in the box below.

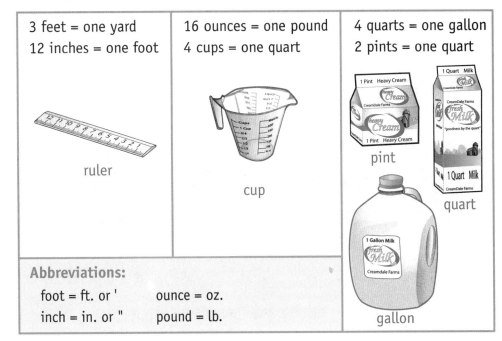

3 feet = one yard
12 inches = one foot

ruler

16 ounces = one pound
4 cups = one quart

cup

4 quarts = one gallon
2 pints = one quart

pint

quart

gallon

Abbreviations:

foot = ft. or '   ounce = oz.
inch = in. or "   pound = lb.

EXAMPLE _How many feet are there in a yard? There are 3 feet in a yard._

1. _____

2. _____

3. _____

4. _____

5. _____

EXERCISE 7 Fill in the blanks with the missing words from the box below.

there's	there is	there are
is there	are there ✓	how many

Rick: I'm going for a walk.

Sue: Wait. I need a few things at the supermarket. Let me look at my

shopping list.

Rick: How many things ___*are there*___ on the list?
                              (example)

Sue: About ten. Also go to the office store. We need CDs.

Rick: Where's the office store?

Sue: _____ a few office supply stores near here. _____
              (1)   *(2)*

an office store next to the supermarket on Elm St. Buy a package

of CDs.

Rick: _____ CDs _____ in a package?
              (3)   *(4)*

Sue: You can buy a package of 50.

Rick: _____ anything else on your list?
              (5)

Sue: Yes, _____. We need computer paper for the
                   (6)

printer. Buy five packs of paper.

Rick: _____ sheets of paper _____ in a
              (7)   *(8)*

pack?

Sue: Five hundred, I think.

Rick: I need the car. _____ enough gas in the tank?
(9)

Sue: I don't think so. Fill up the tank too.

EXERCISE 8 Fill in the blanks with the missing words. Use *there is/are* or *is/are there*.

Marta: The kids need new coats. Let's go shopping today. __*There's*__ a
(example)

12-hour sale at Baker's Department Store—today only.

Simon: _____ a sale on men's coats too?
(1)

Marta: Yes, _____. _____ a lot of great things on
(2)   (3)

sale: winter coats, sweaters, boots, gloves—and more.

Simon: How do you always know about all the sales in town?

Marta: It's easy. Look. _____ an ad in the newspaper.
(4)

Simon: It says, "End of winter sale. All winter things 50% off." Why

_____ a sale on winter things? It's still winter.
(5)

Marta: Spring is almost here.

Simon: It's only January. It's so cold. _____ two or three more
(6)

months of winter.

Marta: We think it's winter. But stores need space for new things.

1. Remember: Certain time expressions don't use prepositions.

   Simon works five days ~~in~~ a week.

2. Use the correct preposition.

   at
   Sue likes to shop ~~in the~~ night.

   in
   Your favorite program begins ~~after~~ 20 minutes.

3. Don't use *to* after *near*.

   There's a convenience store near ~~to~~ my house.

4. Don't make a contraction for *there are*.

   There are
   ~~There're~~ 20 students in the class.

5. Don't use *a* after *there are*.

   There are ~~a~~ good sales this week.

6. Don't use a double negative.

   any
   There aren't ~~no~~ lightbulbs in this aisle.

7. Use correct word order.

   are there
   How many batteries ~~there are~~ in the flashlight?

8. Don't make a contraction with a short *yes* answer.

   there is
   Is there an elevator in the store? Yes ~~there's~~.

Find the mistakes with the underlined words, and correct them. Not every sentence has a mistake. If the sentence is correct, write *C*.

EXAMPLES   Rick and Sue are ~~in~~ *at* home now.

Shampoo is <u>on</u> sale this week.   *C*

1. There are <u>a</u> big stores downtown.

2. Stores are crowded <u>at</u> the weekend.

3. It's 8:45. The store closes <u>at</u> 9:00. It closes <u>after</u> 15 minutes.

4. <u>There're</u> many shoppers <u>in</u> the afternoon.

5. <u>There are</u> a lot of children's programs <u>in</u> TV <u>on</u> Saturday mornings.

6. I go to school three days <u>in</u> a week.

7. There is <u>a</u> big store <u>near to</u> my house.

8. Is there a clerk in aisle 3? Yes, <u>there's</u>.

9. How many convenience stores <u>there are</u> in this city?

10. <u>There's</u> coffee <u>at</u> aisle four.

11. <u>There</u> aren't <u>no</u> clerks on the second floor.

12. Bread is on sale: two <u>for</u> one.

1. What did you learn in this unit? Write three sentences in your notebook about each of these topics:
   - Shopping in the United States
   - Different types of stores
   - Getting a good price
2. Write three questions you still have about shopping in the U.S.

EXPANSION ACTIVITIES

Writing Activity

In your notebook, write five or six sentences to describe each picture.

Outside Activity

Check your local newspaper for ads for your favorite pharmacy or supermarket. Find a product that's on sale. What is the sale price? Find a product with a coupon. What is the sale price with the coupon? Write about the ads in your notebook.

Internet Activities

1. Search the words *metric conversion* on a search engine. Choose a Web site. Find your weight and height in both metric and American measurements.

2. Find the Web site of a big office supply store. Find the price of a package of printer paper.

UNIT

8

GRAMMAR

The Present Continuous Tense
Time Expressions

CONTEXT

Errands

LESSON 1

GRAMMAR

Present Continuous Tense—Affirmative Statements
Spelling of the *-ing* Form of the Verb
Uses of the Present Continuous Tense
Present Continuous Tense—Negative Forms
Expressions of Time with the Present Continuous Tense

CONTEXT

At the Post Office

Before You Read

1. What services does the U.S. post office have? What items does the post office sell?

2. Do you send packages to your country? Why or why not?

AT THE POST OFFICE

It is Saturday morning. People **are doing** errands. They **aren't wearing** their work clothes. They**'re wearing** casual clothes. Many things **are happening** at the post office. The postal clerks are very busy. Many people **are waiting** in line. They**'re not getting** fast service today. But they **aren't complaining.** Halina and Dorota are first in line. Halina's daughter, Anna, is with her.

A customer at the counter has two packages. The clerk **is weighing** one package. He**'s using** a scale. The man **is holding** the other package. He **isn't paying** for the postage in cash. He**'s using** his credit card.

Marta **is picking up** a package. Amy is with her. Amy **is holding** Marta's hand. The clerk **is checking** Marta's identification (ID).

A customer **is using** the automated postal center. He **isn't waiting** in line. He**'s mailing** a package and he**'s weighing** the package on the scale. He**'s paying** by credit card. The machine **is printing** the postage label. Self-service is fast.

A customer **is buying** stamps from a stamp machine. He**'s paying** in cash. He**'s not using** coins. He**'s putting** a ten-dollar bill in the stamp machine. Stamp machines in the post office give coins for change. This man **is getting** some one-dollar coins in change. Nobody **is buying** phone cards or mailing supplies today.

Vocabulary in Context

do errand(s)	She's **doing errands** today. She's going to the post office and the supermarket.
customer(s)	The **customers** are waiting in the post office.
postal clerk(s)	The **postal clerks** are are helping the customers.
counter	The clerks work behind the **counter** at the post office.
casual clothes	We can play or relax in **casual clothes**.
pick up	One customer is **picking up** her package. She is getting it from the clerk.
weigh	The clerk is **weighing** a customer's package. The package **weighs** two pounds.
scale	We use a **scale** to weigh things.
postage	When we mail a package, we have to pay **postage.**
automated postal center	We can weigh our packages, print postage, and pay at the **automated postal center.** We don't need a clerk.

Did You Know? The U.S. made its first stamps in 1847. They cost 5 cents. Today people send more than 202 billion pieces of mail each year.

Listening Activity

Listen to the sentences about the activities in the post office. Circle *true* or *false*.

EXAMPLE (TRUE)　FALSE

1. TRUE FALSE		5. TRUE FALSE	
2. TRUE FALSE		6. TRUE FALSE	
3. TRUE FALSE		7. TRUE FALSE	
4. TRUE FALSE		8. TRUE FALSE	

8.1 | Present Continuous Tense—Affirmative Statements

Subject	*Be*	Verb + *-ing*	Complement
I	**am**	**waiting**	in line.
He	**is**	**mailing**	a letter.
Nobody	**is**	**wearing**	work clothes.
We	**are**	**using**	the stamp machine.
You	**are**	**picking up**	a package.
They	**are**	**standing**	behind the counter.

Language Notes:

1. We can make contractions with a pronoun + *be*.
   I'm waiting in line.
   He's mailing a letter.
   We're using the stamp machine.
2. We can make contractions with a singular noun + *is*.
   Halina's waiting in line.
3. There is no contraction for a plural noun + *are*.
   The **clerks are** standing behind the counter.

EXERCISE **1** Fill in the blanks with the affirmative present continuous tense. Use contractions where possible. Use the ideas from the reading and the verbs in the box below. Use one verb twice.

mail	wear	show	weigh	help	stand	buy ✓	wait

EXAMPLE One customer *'s buying* some stamps.

1. Dorota _____ next to Halina and Anna.

2. Dorota, Halina, and Anna _____ in line.

3. Marta _____ her ID to the postal clerk.

4. Nobody _____ phone cards.

5. The clerks _____ the customers.

6. A customer _____ a package at the automated postal center.

7. Everybody _____ casual clothes today.

8. Two clerks _____ behind the counter.

8.2 | Spelling of the *-ing* Form of the Verb

Verb	*-ing* Form	Rule
go eat look	go**ing** eat**ing** look**ing**	In most cases, add *-ing* to the base form.
sit plan	sit**ting** plan**ning**	If the verb ends in consonant + vowel + consonant, double the last consonant. Then add *-ing*.
give write	giv**ing** writ**ing**	If the verb ends in a consonant + *e*, take off the *e*. Then add *-ing*. Do not double the last consonant after you take off *e*.
show pay	show**ing** pay**ing**	Do not double final *w, x,* or *y*. Just add *-ing*.

Fill in the blanks with the present continuous of the verb in parentheses ( ). Spell the *-ing* form correctly. Use contractions where possible.

EXAMPLE   She __'s mailing__ (mail) a letter.

1. They _____ (get) some stamps.

2. Halina _____ (wait) with her daughter.

3. The clerk _____ (take) a customer's money.

4. Halina _____ (talk) to Dorota.

5. Two customers _____ (use) machines.

6. A man _____ (put) money in the stamp machine.

7. Nobody _____ (plan) to buy mailing supplies.

8. They _____ (write) an address on the package.

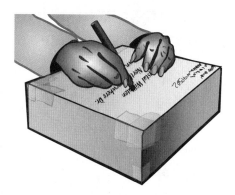

8.3 | Uses of the Present Continuous Tense

Examples	Explanation
People **are buying** stamps now.	The action is happening now, at this time.
She**'s standing** near the stamp machine. He**'s wearing** casual clothes today. They**'re holding** hands. Nobody**'s sitting** on the floor.	There is no action, but we use the present continuous with these common verbs: *stand, sleep, sit, wear, hold,* and *wait.*
I'm working overtime this week.	We use the present continuous when the action is happening during a specific time period.

3 Write two sentences about each picture. Write about what is happening now in the picture. Use verbs from the box below.

stand	wait	wear	play	hold	give	take	write	use
leave	work	pick up	go	buy	put	mail	get	sit

EXAMPLE

This young man is going into the post office. He's wearing casual clothes today.

1.

2.

3.

4.

5.

6.

8.4 | Present Continuous Tense—Negative Forms

Subject	Be	Not	Verb + *-ing*	Complement
I	am	not	getting	mailing supplies.
She	is	not	buying	stamps.
The woman	is	not	using	the stamp machine.
We	are	not	wearing	work clothes.
You	are	not	planning	to go to the post office.
They	are	not	writing	the correct address.
The women	are	not	driving	to the post office.

Language Notes:

1. We can make negative contractions with *be*.

 I'm not getting mailing supplies.

 The **woman's not** using the stamp machine.

 You aren't planning to go to the post office.

2. Do not make a contraction with a plural noun and *are*.

 The women aren't driving to the post office.

EXERCISE **4** Rewrite each sentence below. Make a negative sentence by changing the subject or verb. Use the words given.

EXAMPLE Marta is waiting with Amy. (talk to Amy now)
She's not talking to Amy now. OR *She isn't talking to Amy now.*

1. A man is buying stamps. (buy a phone card)

 _____

2. Many people are waiting in line. (Marta)

 _____

3. Halina and Dorota are waiting for service. (get mailing supplies)

 _____

4. The clerks are working today. (take the day off)

 _____

5. Halina is doing some errands today. (stay home)

 _____

EXERCISE 5   ABOUT YOU Use the words below to write TRUE sentences about your activities at the present time. Make an affirmative or negative sentence. If you write a negative sentence, write a TRUE affirmative sentence also.

EXAMPLES   I / write in my language
I'm not writing in my language now. I'm writing in English.

We / attend class
We're attending class now.

1. I / sit in a comfortable chair

_____

2. The teacher / wear casual clothes

_____

3. We / work on a computer

_____

4. I / use a pen

_____

5. We / learn about the supermarket

_____

6. All of the students / write the same sentences

_____

7. I / spell all the words correctly

_____

8. The teacher / help me now

_____

8.5 | Expressions of Time with the Present Continuous Tense

Examples	Expressions of Time
I'm not cashing a check **right now.**	now (right now)
The clerk's not helping customers **at the moment.**	at the moment
We're working at home **today.** We're working at home **all day.**	today all day
They're not working overtime **this week.** I'm not working **at this time.**	this week (this month) at this time

EXERCISE **6** Complete the short conversations with an affirmative or negative present continuous verb. Circle the expressions of time.

EXAMPLE   A: Can I use your computer?

B: Sorry, I __'m using__ it (at the moment). Can you wait?
           (use)

1. A: Can you mail this letter for me?

   B: Sorry, I _____ home all day today.
                        (stay)

      I _____ to the post office.
            (go)

2. A: Dorota can't do these errands for you now.

   B: Why not?

   A: She can't use her car this week. She _____
                                                    (have)
      problems with it.

3. A: Victor doesn't have time to help you after work.

   B: Why not?

   A: He _____ overtime this week.
              (work)

4. A: Please don't use the phone right now.

   B: Why not?

   A: Because I _____ an important call.
                      (expect)

5. A: What's wrong with this stamp machine?

   B: I don't know. But it _____ right today.
                                 (work)

6. A: This post office is very busy right now.

   B: Yes. A lot of people _____ in line at the counter.
                                  (wait)

EXERCISE 7 Marta has her package now. She's leaving the post office. She sees Dorota and Halina. Read their conversation. Then make true sentences about the conversation with the words given. Use the present continuous tense, affirmative and negative.

Marta: Hi, Dorota. It's nice to see you, Halina. How are you?

Halina: I'm fine. It's good to see you, Marta.

Dorota: Hi, Marta. I'm mailing this package to my son. He's in college now. He's living in Canada. As usual, this line is moving too slowly.

Marta: The post office has services online now. The Web site has prices for all packages. You can print the postage. You can pay for it online with your credit card. Then you can give the package to your mail carrier the next day. The cost is the same. And it's fast!

Dorota: I know. But I can't weigh the package at home. I don't have a scale. I need to send this package today.

Marta: This post office has a new automated postal center. You can weigh the package and pay for postage from a machine now. It's over there. And nobody's waiting.

Dorota: I don't know how to use it. Can you help me?

EXAMPLE Marta and Dorota / talk

Marta and Dorota are talking about post office services.

Marta and Dorota aren't talking to Amy now.

1. Dorota / tell / Marta

_____

_____

2. Dorota / complain

_____

_____

3. The line / move very fast

_____

_____

4. Dorota / send

_____

_____

5. Halina and Dorota / wait

_____

_____

LESSON 2

GRAMMAR

Yes/No Questions with the Present Continuous Tense
Information Questions with the Present Continuous Tense
Question Words as Subjects

CONTEXT

The Drive-Through

Before You Read

1. Where are the drive-throughs in your neighborhood?
2. Which drive-throughs do you use?

tube

microphone

THE DRIVE-THROUGH

Americans do a lot of errands from their cars. They use drive-throughs. Marta and Amy are at their bank drive-through now.

Amy: **Are we going** home now, Mommy?

Marta: Not yet. I still have a few errands.

Amy: **Where are we going** now?

Marta: To the bank. I need some quarters for the washing machine. I can get a roll of 40 quarters for $10 at the bank.

Amy: **Why are you turning** here, Mommy? The bank's over there.

Marta: I'm using the drive-through, and the entrance is here.

Amy: There's someone ahead of us. **What's she doing? Is she getting** quarters, too?

Marta: She's getting money. But not quarters. She's probably cashing a check.

Amy: **Who's talking?** I hear a voice.

Marta: That's the teller. She's behind the window. She's using a microphone.

Amy: **What's that man doing** over there?

Marta: He's sending a deposit to the teller at the window. There's money or checks in that envelope.

Amy: **What's he holding?**

Marta: It's a tube. It's a place for his deposit. He can put checks or cash in the tube, and a machine takes the tube to the teller.

Amy: **Is the teller helping** both customers at the same time?

Marta: Yes.

Vocabulary in Context

drive-through	Marta and Amy are using a **drive-through.** They don't have to get out of the car for service.
tube	A customer is using a **tube** to send a deposit to the teller.
entrance	Amy's mom is going into the **entrance** of the drive-through.
roll	You can get a **roll** of 40 quarters at a bank.
turn	They are **turning** into the entrance.
teller	A **teller** is helping a customer at the bank.
microphone	The teller is using a **microphone** to talk to people.
probably	That customer is **probably** making a deposit. I'm not sure.
ahead of	Three people are **ahead of** us in line. We have to wait.

Many places often have drive-throughs.
- banks
- restaurants
- pharmacies

Listening Activity

Listen to the following questions about the conversation. Circle *true* or *false*.

EXAMPLE (TRUE)   FALSE

1. TRUE   FALSE   5. TRUE   FALSE

2. TRUE   FALSE   6. TRUE   FALSE

3. TRUE   FALSE   7. TRUE   FALSE

4. TRUE   FALSE   8. TRUE   FALSE

8.6 | *Yes/No* Questions with the Present Continuous Tense

Be	Subject	Verb + -*ing*	Complement	Short Answer
Am	I	**using**	the right window?	Yes, you are.
Are	you	**talking**	to the teller?	Yes, I am.
Is	Halina	**going**	into the bank?	No, she isn't.
Are	we	**turning**	here?	No, we're not.
Are	they	**getting**	some quarters?	Yes, they are.

EXERCISE 1   Make a *yes/no* question with the words given. Answer the question with a short answer. Use the ideas from the conversation.

EXAMPLE   Amy / talk to Marta

Is Amy talking to Marta? Yes, she is.

_____

1. Marta and Amy / wait in the car

_____

2. the man / ask for a roll of quarters

_____

3. the teller / help Marta

_____

4. the customers / complain about the service

_____

5. Marta and Amy / use the drive-through

_____

6. the tube / take a deposit to the teller

_____

7. the teller / talk to a customer

_____

8. Marta / answer Amy's questions

_____

EXERCISE 2 ABOUT YOU Use the words given to ask a partner questions about his or her present time activities. Your partner will answer with a short answer first and then add information. Write the questions and answers for practice.

EXAMPLE (you / speak English)

A: _Are you speaking English now?_

B: _Yes, I am. I'm using the present continuous tense._

1. you / listen to the teacher

_____

_____

2. you / practice the simple present tense

_____

_____

3. you / use a Web site

_____

_____

4. your classmates / take a test

_____

_____

5. you / write in your book

_____

_____

6. your teacher / stand in front of the class

_____

_____

7. you / learn / a lot of new words today

_____

_____

8. your classmates / talk to you

_____

_____

8.7 | Information Questions with the Present Continuous Tense

Question Word	*Be*	Subject	Verb + *-ing* + Complement	Short Answer
What	**are**	you	**doing?**	Waiting for service.
Where	**is**	he	**going?**	To the drive-through.
How many people	**is**	the teller	**helping?**	Just one right now.
Why	**are**	we	**waiting?**	Because the teller is busy.
Who	**are**	they	**talking** to?	The teller.
Why	**are**	Amy and Marta	**using** the drive-through?	Because it's easy and fast.

Write questions for the answers given. Use the question words: *who, what, where, why, how many,* and *how.* The underlined word or phrase is the answer.

EXAMPLE   *What is Amy asking Marta?*

Amy's asking Marta <u>about the drive-through</u>.

1. _____

   The teller is talking to <u>a customer</u>.

2. _____

   Marta is waiting <u>to get some quarters</u> at the bank.

3. _____

   Marta is expecting to get <u>40 quarters</u>.

4. _____

   The customer is putting a bank deposit <u>in a tube</u>.

5. _____

   The teller is talking to customers <u>with a microphone</u>.

6. _____

   The teller is helping <u>only one</u> customer at the moment.

7. _____

   Marta and Amy are talking about <u>the other customers</u>.

8.8 | Question Words as Subjects

Subject	Be	Verb Phrase	Short Answer
Who	**is**	**talking?**	Amy and Marta.
What	**is**	**happening** at the bank?	Customers are doing business.
Which customer	**is**	**waiting** in line?	Marta.
How many customers	**are**	**waiting** for service?	Just one.

Language Notes:

1. Use a plural verb (*are*) after *how many*, even if the answer is singular.
2. Use a singular verb (*is*) after *who*, even if the answer is plural.

EXERCISE 4 Make questions for each answer given. The underlined word or phrase is the answer. Use the question words *who*, *which*, *what*, and *how many* as subjects.

EXAMPLE *Which customer is using the tube?*

A <u>man</u> is using the tube.

1. _____

   The <u>teller</u> is using a microphone.

2. _____

   <u>One</u> customer is using the tube.

3. _____

   <u>A man and a woman</u> are getting help now.

4. _____

   <u>Nothing</u> is happening at the ATM.

5. _____

   <u>Three</u> customers are using the drive-through.

6. _____

   <u>A tube</u> is taking the man's deposit to the teller.

EXERCISE 5 Complete the conversation between Marta and Amy at the fast food drive-through. Use the words and expressions in the box.

are waiting	he's asking	is putting
what are you getting	are we going	is it doing ✓

Amy: Mommy, the sign is talking. How _____*is it doing*_____ that?
(example)

Marta: It's not the sign. It's the clerk. Look. He's over there at the

pick-up window. _____(1)_____ for our order.

Amy: What are you getting, Mommy?

Marta: A burger and fries. Maybe a salad. _____(2)_____, Amy?

Amy: Ummmmmm.

Marta: Hurry, Amy, the clerk's waiting. And customers

_____(3)_____ behind us.

Amy: Ummmm. A burger and a shake.

Marta: *(speaking to the clerk)* Two burgers, a small order of fries, and a chocolate shake, please.

Clerk: That's $7.79 with tax.

Amy: _____ to the pick-up window now?
                    (4)

Marta: Yes. Look. The clerk _____ our lunch in a bag.
                                              (5)

Clerk: Two dollars and 21 cents is your change. Thank you. Have a good day.

EDITING ADVICE

1. Always use a form of *be* with the present continuous tense.

   is
   He ˄working at that store.

2. Use the correct word order in a question.

   is he
   What ~~he is~~ doing there?

3. Don't use the present continuous for usual or customary actions.

   rent
   Video stores ~~are renting~~ videos to many people.

4. Don't forget to put *-ing* on the end of present continuous verbs.

   ing
   They *are go* ˄ to the movies today.

EDITING QUIZ

Find the mistakes with the underlined words, and correct them. If the sentence is correct, write *C*.

He's not
EXAMPLES   ~~He not~~ going to the video store today.

She <u>likes</u> her work.   *C*

1. We <u>are going</u> to the bank every week.

2. How many packages <u>he is weighing</u>?

3. Many customers <u>buying</u> stamps from the machine.

4. He <u>isn't writing</u> the correct address.

5. Why <u>they waiting</u> in their car?

6. Those people <u>are mailing</u> letters every Saturday.

7. How much cash is he <u>deposit</u> now?

1. What did you learn in this unit? Write three sentences in your notebook about each topic.
   - U.S. post office services
   - Drive-through windows

2. Write three questions you still have about the post office or banks in the United States.

EXPANSION ACTIVITIES

Writing Activity

In your notebook, write five or six sentences about what is or isn't happening in the picture.

EXAMPLE *Simon is working on his computer. He isn't going to the post office today.*

Outside Activities

1. Go to a post office in your city. Bring a package to weigh. Ask how much it costs to send the package to your home country (you don't have to send it). If the post office has an automated postal center, use it to weigh the package and find the price.

2. Look for mailing supplies at the post office. Find out how much a small box or a large mailing envelope costs.

3. Go to a fast food restaurant in your neighborhood. Does it have a drive-through? Write some sentences about what is happening.

Internet Activities

1. Go to the Web site of a bank in your area. Find out how to open an online account.

2. Go to the United States Postal Service Web site (www.usps.gov). Find out how to buy stamps. Find out how to send a package to your country.

UNIT

9

GRAMMAR

The Future Tense with *Be Going To*
Expressions of Time in the Future

CONTEXT

Making Changes

LESSON

GRAMMAR

Affirmative Statements with *Be Going To*
Negative Statements with *Be Going To*
Uses of the Future Tense with *Be Going To*
Expressions of Time with *Be Going To*

CONTEXT

Getting Ready for a New Baby

Before You Read

1. What do parents have to buy for a new baby?
2. What changes in family life are necessary for a new baby?

stroller   high chair   crib

GETTING READY FOR A NEW BABY

Shafia and her husband, Ali, **are going to have** a baby. Dorota and Halina are visiting Shafia. Ali is at work.

Shafia: My baby**'s going to arrive** in two months. I'm not ready.

Dorota: Let's see. You**'re going to need** a crib, a high chair, and a car seat.

Halina: You can use my daughter's crib. She's two now and she has a bigger bed. She**'s not going to need** the crib anymore.

Shafia: That's wonderful, Halina, thank you. I**'m not going to need** a car seat for a while. We don't have a car right now.

Dorota: Then you**'re going to need** a stroller to take the baby outside. There's a resale shop for kids in my neighborhood. You can get a high chair and a stroller there. Resale shops are not expensive.

Shafia: What's a resale shop, Dorota?

Dorota: It's a store with used items. People take their used clothing and furniture there. The shop sells them at a low price. The money often goes to a charity. Resale shops are very popular.

Shafia: That's a great idea. We can go on Thursday.

Dorota: That's fine. But don't buy too many clothes for the baby. People **are going to give** you gifts.

Shafia: You're right. We have a lot of relatives. We**'re not going to buy** too much.

Halina: You**'re** also **going to need** some help for the first weeks. New babies are a lot of work. And you**'re not going to get** much sleep.

Shafia: I know. My mother**'s going to help**. She**'s going to stay** with us for the first month. She's so excited. She**'s going to be** a grandmother for the first time.

Vocabulary in Context

used	This furniture is not new. It is **used.**
crib	Babies sleep in **cribs.**
stroller	You can take a baby for a walk in a **stroller.**
resale shop	We can buy good used items at a **resale shop.** Resale shops are sometimes called "thrift stores."
for a while	She's going to stay here **for a while.** I don't know how long.
furniture	She needs baby **furniture:** a bed and a high chair.
charity	She gives money to a **charity.** The charity helps sick children.
relative	She is my husband's sister. She is a **relative** of our family.
excited	We are **excited** about the baby. We are very happy.

Did You Know? In the U.S., women between the ages of 20 and 30 have fewer babies today than in past years. But women between the ages of 35 and 44 have more.

Listening Activity Listen to the sentences about the conversation. Circle *true* or *false*.

EXAMPLE (TRUE)   FALSE

1. TRUE   FALSE   5. TRUE   FALSE
2. TRUE   FALSE   6. TRUE   FALSE
3. TRUE   FALSE   7. TRUE   FALSE
4. TRUE   FALSE   8. TRUE   FALSE

9.1 | Affirmative Statements with *Be Going To*

Subject	Be	Going To	Verb (Base Form)	Complement
I	am	going to	need	some help.
My mother	is	going to	help	me.
We	are	going to	have	a baby.
You	are	going to	give	us a crib.
They	are	going to	buy	a used high chair.
My relatives	are	going to	give	us gifts.
There	is	going to	be	a change in Shafia's life.

Language Notes:

1. We can make contractions with the subject + *be*.

   I'm going to need some help.

   My **mother's** going to help me.

   They're going to buy us a gift.

   There's going to be a new resale shop in this area.

2. We don't make a contraction with a plural subject + *are*.

   My relatives **are** going to give us gifts.

3. In normal speech, we pronounce *going to* / gənə /. Listen to your teacher pronounce the sentences in the chart above.

EXERCISE 1 Fill in the blanks with the affirmative of the verb in parentheses ( ). Use the future tense with *be going to*.

EXAMPLE She <u>'s going to get</u> some things for the baby.
(get)

1. Halina and Dorota _____ Shafia again on Thursday.
   (see)

2. Shafia's mother _____ her with the new baby.
   (help)

3. The new baby _____ soon.
   (arrive)

4. Shafia's relatives _____ a lot of gifts for the baby.
   (bring)

5. Halina and Dorota _____ Shafia to the resale shop.
   (take)

6. Shafia _____ a stroller for the baby.
   (need)

7. Shafia and Ali _____ parents for the first time.
   (be)

8. With the help of her friends, Shafia _____ ready
   (be)
   for the baby.

9.2 | Negative Statements with *Be Going To*

Subject	Form of *Be* + Not	*Going To*	Verb (Base Form)	Complement
I	**am not**	**going to**	**need**	help.
My father	**is not**	**going to**	**help**	me.
We	**are not**	**going to**	**have**	a boy.
You	**are not**	**going to**	**give**	us a stroller.
Those people	**are not**	**going to**	**buy**	us a gift.
There	**are not**	**going to**	**be**	many people at the shop.

Language Notes:

1. We can make contractions with negative forms of *be*.
   I'm not going to need help.
   My **father's not** going to help me.
   You aren't going to give us a stroller.
   There isn't going to be time to shop today.

2. We don't use a contraction with a plural noun + *are*.
   Those people **aren't** going to give us a gift.

Fill in the blanks with the negative form of *be going to*. Use the verbs in parentheses ( ). Use contractions where possible.

EXAMPLE Shafia <u>*isn't going to buy*</u> a lot of baby clothes.
(buy)

1. With a new baby, Shafia and Ali _____ a lot of sleep.
(get)

2. Shafia's mother _____ a year.
(stay)

3. Shafia _____ a car seat for a while.
(need)

4. Dorota, Halina, and Shafia _____ at the resale store today.
(shop)

5. There _____ enough space for all the baby furniture in
(be)

   their apartment.

6. Relatives _____ Shafia a crib.
(give)

7. The resale shop _____ open on Sunday.
(be)

8. Shafia _____ a lot of baby clothes.
(buy)

9. Ali _____ Shafia to the resale shop.
(take)

9.3 | Uses of the Future Tense with *Be Going To*

Examples	Explanation
Shafia**'s going to buy** some things for the baby.	We use *be going to* with future plans.
You**'re not going to get** much sleep.	We use *be going to* with predictions for the future.
Language Note: We often shorten *going to go* to *going to*. We're **going to** the resale shop next week.	

EXERCISE **3** Fill in the blanks with the affirmative or negative form of *be going to* and the verb in parentheses ( ). Use the ideas from the conversation.

EXAMPLE Halina and Dorota <u>*are going to help*</u> Shafia.
(help)

1. Shafia _____ a crib.
(buy)

2. Shafia's mother _____ a grandmother.
(be)

3. Halina _____ Shafia a car seat.
   (give)

4. Shafia _____ a high chair at the resale shop.
   (get)

5. Shafia, Halina, and Dorota _____ to the resale shop on
   (go)

   Thursday.

6. Shafia's baby _____ in two months.
   (arrive)

7. There _____ a new person in Shafia's house.
   (be)

8. The new baby _____ a lot of gifts.
   (get)

9. There _____ many changes in Shafia and Ali's house.
   (be)

9.4 | Expressions of Time with *Be Going To*

Time expressions in the future can go at the beginning or end of the sentence.
Learn the prepositions with each expression of time.

Examples	Explanation
She's going to visit me **in** two weeks. **In** two weeks, she's going to visit me. She's going to visit me **in** January. They're going to visit **in** 2010.	We use *in* with numbers of days, weeks, months, or years in the future. It means **after**. We use *in* with names of months or years.
I'm going to visit you **on** January 12.	We use *on* with dates.
On Thursday, I'm going shopping. I'm going shopping **this** Thursday.	We use *on* or *this* with names of days. **This** means a future day in a present week.
I'm going to get some new clothes **this** week.	We use *this* with future time in the same week, month, or year.
Tomorrow I can help you. I can't help you **tonight**.	We use *tomorrow* for the day after today. *Tonight* means this night.
They're going to visit us **next week**.	We use *next* with weeks, months, or years after the present week, month, or year.
She's going to stay with us **for a while**.	*For a while* means for an indefinite amount of time.
She's going to live here **for** a month.	We use *for* with a specific amount of time.
We're going to see our relatives **soon**.	We use *soon* for a near future time that is not specific.

EXERCISE 4 Fill in the blanks with the correct preposition for each expression of time.

EXAMPLE I'm going to be 23 years old ____*on*____ February 16.

1. Shafia's going to have her baby _____ two months.

2. Shafia's going to visit the resale shop _____ week.

3. Shafia and Ali are going to stay in their apartment _____ a while.

4. Shafia's mother is going to stay _____ a month.

5. We're going to take a vacation _____ August.

6. I'm going to do the laundry _____ Saturday.

7. He's going to go back to his country _____ 2020.

8. Their relatives are going to arrive _____ September 22.

EXERCISE 5 ABOUT YOU Write a sentence about your future plans. Use the verbs given in the future with *be going to*. Use an expression of time.

EXAMPLE have dinner with my Mom

I'm going to have dinner with my Mom next Sunday.

1. do my homework for this class

   _____

2. get a (different) job

   _____

3. finish this book

   _____

4. go to the supermarket

   _____

5. come to English class again

   _____

6. have a test in this class

   _____

7. use a computer

   _____

January

Sunday	Monday	Tuesday	
1	2	3 Today	4
8	9 dinner with Mom	10	11
15 Party at Jan's	16	17 Doctor's appt.	18

8. go to my next class

_____

9. speak English very well

_____

EXERCISE **6** ABOUT YOU Make predictions about your future. Think about your life in ten years. Use the verbs given in the affirmative or negative with _be going to_. Add information where possible.

EXAMPLE live in an apartment

In ten years, I'm not going to live in an apartment.

I'm going to have a house.

1. live in this city

_____

_____

2. be a student

_____

_____

3. work in an office

_____

_____

4. have a big family

_____

_____

5. be a U.S. citizen

_____

_____

6. forget my language

_____

_____

7. return to my country to live

_____

_____

8. have a different car

_____

_____

EXERCISE **7** Complete the conversations. Use the verbs given in the affirmative or negative with _be going to_.

Conversation A:

Halina and Shafia are talking about the new baby's room.

Halina: Where is the new baby's room?

Shafia: We have an extra room. It's small. But there ____is going to be____
(example: be)

enough space for a crib.

Halina: What's in the room now?

Shafia: There's a desk and a computer. But we _____
(1. keep)

them there. Ali _____ them to the living room
(2. move)

next month. His brother _____ him. The desk
(3. help)

is very heavy.

Halina: What about the color of the walls?

Shafia: We _____ the room pink. But not now. There
(4. paint)

_____ enough time.
(5. be)

Conversation B:

Halina, Dorota, and Shafia are talking about the baby's name.

Halina: Shafia, do you have a name for the baby?

Shafia: No. Ali and I _____ a name later. We
                                         (1. choose)

_____. It's very important to choose the right
(2. hurry)

name. After the baby's birth, we _____ some of
                                                    (3. ask)

our relatives for ideas.

Dorota: There are long lists of names on the Web. Just search "baby names." You can even find the meaning of each name.

Shafia: That's interesting. But the baby _____ an
                                                          (4. have)

American name. We _____ the baby a name
                                  (5. give)

from our country.

Dorota: There are names from other countries on the Web too. There are thousands of names for boys and girls.

Shafia: Thanks, Dorota. But we _____ to see the baby
                                                 (6. wait)

first.

LESSON 2

GRAMMAR

Yes/No Questions with *Be Going To*
Information Questions with *Be Going To*
Questions with *How Long* and *Be Going To*
Subject Questions with *Be Going To*

CONTEXT

Moving to a New Apartment

Before You Read

1. Are you going to move soon? Why or why not?

2. How do people prepare for a move?

MOVING TO A NEW APARTMENT

Victor: I'm going to move in two weeks. There's so much to do!
Simon: You're right. **Are you going to hire** a mover?
Victor: No, I'm not. I'm going to rent a truck. We don't have a lot of things. But I'm going to need some help. **Are you going to be** available on the 25th of this month?
Simon: Sure. I can help you.
Victor: Thanks, Simon. What should I do about my mail?
Simon: You can fill out a change-of-address card at the post office. Or, you can fill it out online. It's easy to do. The post office sends your mail to your new address for one year.
Victor: **What's going to happen** with my phone?
Simon: You have to call the phone company. **Is your new apartment going to be** in the same neighborhood?
Victor: Yes, it is. Why?
Simon: Then you can probably keep the same phone number.
Victor: That's good. **How long is it going to take** for the new service?
Simon: You can usually get it on the same day. There's a fee to change phone service from one place to another. But it's not usually more than $50.
Simon: **When are you going to pack? Are you going to need** boxes?
Victor: I'm starting to pack now. I have some boxes, but not enough.
Simon: Go to some stores in your neighborhood. You can ask them for their old boxes.
Victor: That's a good idea. I also have a lot of old things. **What am I going to do** with them? I don't want to move them.
Simon: You can give them to charity. There's a resale shop in this neighborhood.

Vocabulary in Context

move	Our apartment is too small. We're going to **move** to a bigger apartment.
mover	A **mover** can help you move things from one building to another.
hire	He isn't going to **hire** movers. He doesn't want to pay money to move.
pack	I'm going to **pack** my things. I'm going to put them in boxes.
truck	You can move all your furniture in a moving **truck.**
rent	I can **rent** a truck for one day. It's not expensive.
neighborhood	Victor is moving close to his old apartment. His new apartment is in the same **neighborhood.**
fee	He pays a **fee** for service.

Many Americans move every year. But the number is going down. Only 14 percent of Americans moved in 2003. It was the lowest number since 1948.

 **Listening Activity** Listen to the sentences about the conversation. Circle *true* or *false*.

EXAMPLE   TRUE   (FALSE)

1. TRUE   FALSE   5. TRUE   FALSE

2. TRUE   FALSE   6. TRUE   FALSE

3. TRUE   FALSE   7. TRUE   FALSE

4. TRUE   FALSE

9.5 | *Yes/No* Questions with *Be Going To*

Be	Subject	Going To	Verb (Base Form)	Complement	Short Answer
Am	I	**going to**	**need**	a change of address form?	Yes, you are.
Is	Victor	**going to**	**move**	out of town?	No, he isn't.
Are	we	**going to**	**get**	a new phone number?	No, you aren't.
Are	Victor and Lisa	**going to**	**hire**	a moving company?	No, they aren't.
Is	there	**going to**	**be**	a fee?	Yes, there is.
Are	there	**going to**	**be**	any problems?	Yes, there are.

EXERCISE 1   Write *yes/no* questions about Victor and Simon's conversation. Use *be going to* and the words given. Give a short answer.

EXAMPLE   Victor / move soon

Is Victor going to move soon? Yes, he is.

1. Victor / rent a truck

_____

2. Victor / buy some boxes

_____

3. Victor's new apartment / be in his old neighborhood

_____

4. Victor / change his phone number

_____

5. it / take a long time to get new phone service

_____

6. the post office / send Victor's mail to his new address

_____

7. there / be / a fee to change phone service

_____

8. Victor / move / all his things

_____

EXERCISE 2   Complete the short conversations. Write a *yes/no* question with *be going to*. Use the words in parentheses ( ).

EXAMPLE   **A:** We're going to move.

B: *Are you going to move this week?*
         (this week)

1. **A:** I'm going to change my address.

   B: _____
            (your phone number too)

2. **A:** He's going to pay for that service.

   B: _____
            (more than $50)

3. **A:** They're going to move.

    B: _____
    (to a house)

4. **A:** We're going to visit our relatives.

    B: _____
    (on Saturday)

5. **A:** She's going to get some used furniture.

    B: _____
    (used clothing too)

6. **A:** I'm going to look for a new apartment.

    B: _____
    (in this same neighborhood)

7. **A:** Victor's going to fill out a change-of-address card.

    B: _____
    (online)

9.6 | Information Questions with *Be Going To*

Question Word	*Be*	Subject	*Going To*	Verb (Base Form) + Complement	Short Answer
Why	**are**	you	**going to**	**move?**	Because I need a bigger apartment.
Where	**is**	she	**going to**	**live?**	In California.
Who	**is**	he	**going to**	**hire?**	Ace Moving Company.
When	**are**	they	**going to**	**hire** the movers?	Next week.
How much	**are**	they	**going to**	**pay** them?	About $500.
How many boxes	**are**	there	**going to**	**be?**	Maybe 50 or more.
What kind of fee	**is**	there	**going to**	**be?**	A service fee of $50.

EXERCISE 3 Ask an information question about each statement. Use the question words in parentheses ( ).

EXAMPLE A: He's going to fill out a change-of-address card. (Where)

B: _Where is he going to fill it out?_

1. A: She's going to hire movers. (How many)

   B: _____

2. A: I'm going to get a new phone. (What kind of)

   B: _____

3. A: There are going to be some problems. (What kind of)

   B: _____

4. A: Her relatives are going to come here. (Why)

   B: _____

5. A: You're going to pay a lot for this service. (How much)

   B: _____

6. A: He's going to talk to someone about a new apartment. (Who)

   B: _____

7. A: They're going to help you. (How)

   B: _____

8. A: We're going to change our phone service. (When)

   B: _____

EXERCISE 4 Look at the short answer to each question below. Then ask a question with the words given. Use the correct question word with *be going to*.

EXAMPLE A: _When are you going to move?_
                              (you / move)

B: In about two weeks.

1. A: _____
                    (she / rent the truck)

   B: Next Saturday.

2. A: _____
                  (they / pay for new phone service)

   B: Less than $50.

3. A: _____
                         (he / move)

   B: Because his apartment is too small.

4. A: _____
                         (you / call)

   B: My relatives.

5. A: _____
                       (she / get boxes)

   B: From a store in the neighborhood.

6. A: _____
                         (they / get)

   B: A large, three-bedroom apartment.

7. A: _____
                        (they / pack)

   B: They're going to pack 50 boxes.

9.7 | Questions with *How Long* and *Be Going To*

Examples	Explanation
A: **How long** are you going to stay? B: **Until** next week.	We use *how long* to ask about specific amounts of time. We can use *until* in answers to **how long** questions.
A: **How long** are they going to wait? B: **For** 15 minutes.	We can use *for* in answers to **how long** questions.

EXERCISE 5 ABOUT YOU Ask your partner a question with *How long* for each statement given. Your partner can give an answer with *for* or *until*. Write the questions and answers.

EXAMPLE   you / be in this course

How long are you going to be in this course?

I'm going to be in this course until the end of the semester.

1. we / work on this exercise

2. we / use this book

3. you / stay at school today

4. you / work today

5. this school / be open today

6. you / watch TV tonight

9.8 | Subject Questions with *Be Going To*

Question Word (Subject)	Be	Going To	Verb (Base Form)	Complement	Short Answer
Who	is	going to	move?		Victor is.
How many friends	are	going to	help	Victor?	Two.
What kind of people	are	going to	work	with you?	Young people.
Which services	are	going to	change?		Only the phone service.
What	is	going to	happen?		I'm going to move!

EXERCISE 6   Write an information question for each statement. Use the question word in parentheses ( ) as a subject.

EXAMPLE   Somebody is going to visit me. (Who)

Who is going to visit you?

1. Something is going to change. (What)

   _____

2. Many people are going to move this year. (How many)

   _____

3. Some services are going to be expensive. (Which)

   _____

4. Somebody is going to give me some boxes. (Who)

   _____

5. Something is going to happen on Thursday. (What)

   _____

6. A moving company is going to help me. (Which)

   _____

7. Some apartments are going to be available. (What kind of)

   _____

EXERCISE 7 Victor is calling a truck rental company. He wants to rent a truck for his move. Complete Victor's conversation using *yes/no* and information questions with *be going to*. Use the words in parentheses ( ).

Clerk: Avery Truck Rental. How can I help you?

Victor: I need to rent a truck. I'm going to move, and I'm checking prices.

Clerk: _Are you going to use_ the truck in the city or out of town?
   (example: you / use)

Victor: Here in the city.

Clerk: O.K. _____?
   (1. what kind of truck / you / need)

Victor: I don't know.

Clerk: Well, _____?
   (2. how many rooms / you/ move)

Victor: It's a two-bedroom apartment.

Clerk: A 15-foot truck is big enough.

Victor: _____?
   (3. how much / it / cost)

Clerk: _____ on
   (4. you / move)

the weekend or during the week?

Victor: Is there a difference in price?

Clerk: Yes. It's $20 a day more on the weekends.

_____?
   (5. when / you / need the truck)

Victor: Next week. Wednesday or Thursday.

Clerk: _____ it?
   (6. how long / you / need)

Victor: Just one day.

Clerk: O.K. Then it's going to cost $39.00 a day and 99 cents a mile.

EXERCISE 8 Complete the conversation between Victor and Simon. Use questions and statements with *be going to*. Use the verbs from the box below.

are going to help	I'm going to finish	I'm going to invite
are you going to pack	are going to move out	are you going to be

Simon: When _____ the rest of your things?
(1)

Victor: _____ next week.
(2)

Simon: Ed and I can help you on Thursday. I have the day off.

Victor: Thanks. But _____ available on Sunday?
(3)

The people in my new apartment _____ on
(4)

Sunday. We can take some of my things there on Sunday night.

Simon: We're available then. How many other people

_____ you?
(5)

Victor: Just two of my friends. Then later, _____ you
(6)

all for dinner.

EDITING ADVICE

1. Don't write *gonna*. Write *going to*.

   We're ~~gonna~~ get jobs.
   　　going to

2. Always use a form of *be* with *going to*.

   We ˄ going to shop at a resale shop.
   　　're

3. Always use the correct word order in questions.

   Where ~~they are~~ going to work?
   　　are they

4. Use the correct preposition with time expressions.

   We are going to move ~~on~~ two weeks.
   　　　　　　　　　in

EDITING QUIZ

Find the mistakes with the underlined words, and correct them. Not every sentence has a mistake. If the sentence is correct, write *C*.

EXAMPLES　How long ~~you're going~~ to live here?
　　　　　　are you going

　　　　　　He's going to live here until next year.　*C*

1. Shafia's relatives going to give her many gifts.

2. My family's gonna move in April.

3. When she's going to have the baby?

4. He's going to fill out a change-of-address card.

5. We're going to move in January 29.

6. It's going to take a long time.

7. She's going to stay here on a while.

8. What kind of apartment those people going to get?

1. What did you learn in this unit? Write three sentences in your notebook about each topic.
   - Resale / thrift shops
   - Preparing to move
   - Renting a truck
   - Preparing for a new baby

2. Write three questions you still have about moving to a new apartment or house or about preparing for a new baby.

EXPANSION ACTIVITIES

Writing *Activity*

In your notebook, write a paragraph of six to eight sentences about the picture. Write about what is going to happen.

EXAMPLE *Victor is coming out of his apartment building. He is going to put some boxes on the truck.*

Outside *Activities*

1. Call a truck rental company in your city and find out how much it costs to rent a 15-foot truck next Saturday.

2. Find a resale or thrift shop in your neighborhood. Visit the shop and tell the class about your experience.

Internet *Activities*

1. Search the words *moving tips*. Find some advice about moving. Write three sentences. Share them with the class.

2. Search the words *baby names* or *names*. Find an interesting name (or your name) and read about it. What does it mean? Where does it come from? Tell the class about the name.

UNIT

10

GRAMMAR
Comparatives
Superlatives

CONTEXT
Choices

LESSON 1

GRAMMAR

Comparative Forms of Adjectives
Spelling of the *-er* Form
Comparisons with Nouns and Verbs

CONTEXT

Community Colleges

Before You Read

1. Where is the state university in this state?
2. What community colleges do you know about in this area?

COMMUNITY COLLEGES

In the U.S., many students choose to go to a community college. Students can get a two-year certificate or a degree. Some students start at a community college. Then they go to a four-year college or university to get a bachelor's degree.

A four-year university is **more expensive than** a community college. The average tuition at a community college is $2,000 a year. At a four-year state university, it is $11,000 a year. A community college is often **closer** to home **than** a four-year college. Community colleges in big cities often have several campuses.

There are other differences too. A community college often has **smaller** classes than a university. Some university classes can have more than 100 students. And students at a community college are usually **older than** students at a four-year college. The average age of students at a community college is 29. At a university, most students are between the ages of 18 and 24.

Community college students are often **busier** too. Many students have full- or part-time jobs and families. Community colleges are **more convenient than** universities for students with small children. Many community colleges provide child-care services. There are more night and weekend classes too.

An educated person has a **better** chance of finding a good job. Which is **better** for you: a community college or a four-year college?

Vocabulary in Context

bachelor's degree	My brother has four years of college. He has a **bachelor's degree** in French.
certificate	My cousin has a **certificate** from a community college to work with children.
tuition	Students have to pay **tuition** to go to college.
campus	My college has several **campuses.** There is a **campus** near my house. There is another campus downtown.
educated	My father is an **educated** person. He has a bachelor's degree.
provide	The college **provides** many services.
chance	He's very busy this week. He doesn't have a **chance** to rest.

- Not all students at a community college want to get a degree. Some students go there just to learn more English. Others go to attend a certificate program, such as a certified nursing assistant program. Others go to improve their skills, such as computer skills.

- There are different levels of college degrees: associate's degree, bachelor's degree, master's degree, and PhD (or doctorate).

🎧 Listening Activity

Listen to the sentences about the reading. Circle *true* or *false*.

EXAMPLE (TRUE) FALSE

1. TRUE   FALSE   4. TRUE   FALSE
2. TRUE   FALSE   5. TRUE   FALSE
3. TRUE   FALSE   6. TRUE   FALSE

10.1 | Comparative Forms of Adjectives

We can compare two people or things. There are two patterns of comparison and a few irregular forms. We use *than* to complete the comparison.

Pattern	Simple	Comparative	Examples
Pattern 1: After a one-syllable adjective, add *-er*	old tall	old**er** tall**er**	Community college students are **older than** university students.
Pattern 1 with a spelling change: After a two-syllable adjective that ends in *–y*, change *y* to *i* and add *–er*.	busy happy	bus**ier** happ**ier**	Community college students are often **busier than** university students.
Pattern 2: With other two-syllable adjectives and all three-syllable adjectives add *more* before the adjective.	helpful expensive	**more** helpful **more** expensive	University tuition is **more expensive than** community college tuition.
Irregular Adjectives: We change the word completely.	good bad	**better** **worse**	A community college is **better** for me **than** a university. My grade in Biology is **worse than** my grade in Math.

Language Notes:

1. We omit *than* if we do not mention the second item of comparison.

   She is richer than I am, but I am happier.
2. Some two-syllable words can follow both Pattern 1 or Pattern 2.

   common—**more** common OR common**er**
3. We can put *much* before a comparative form.

   Those students are **much younger** than we are.

10.2 | Spelling of the *-er* Form

Simple Adjective	Comparative Adjective	Explanation
old cheap	old**er** cheap**er**	Add *-er* to most adjectives.
big hot	big**ger** hot**ter**	If the adjective ends with consonant-vowel-consonant, double the final consonant before adding *-er*.
nice late	nice**r** late**r**	If the adjective ends in *e*, add *-r* only.
busy easy	bus**ier** eas**ier**	If a two-syllable adjective ends in *y*, change *y* to *i* and add *-er*.

EXERCISE 1 Write the comparative forms of the adjectives. Use correct spelling.

1. convenient _____   6. funny _____   11. kind _____

2. big _____   7. expensive _____   12. mad _____

3. fine _____   8. friendly _____   13. late _____

4. lazy _____   9. hot _____   14. bad _____

5. hard _____   10. good _____

EXERCISE 2 Compare Wilson College and Jackson University using the information below. The numbers in the table go with the numbers in the exercise.

	Wilson College	Jackson University
Example:	Has night and weekend classes	Doesn't have night or weekend classes
1.	$60 per credit hour	$450 per credit hour
2.	Average class size = 16 students	Average class size = 30 students
3.	80 percent of students have jobs	10 percent of students have jobs
4.	Has a day-care center	Doesn't have a day-care center
5.	All classes are in one building.	The campus has more than 60 buildings.
6.	College opened in 1985.	University opened in 1910.
7.	Teachers have a bachelor's degree or master's degree.	Teachers have a master's degree or PhD.

Use the comparative form of one of the adjectives from the choices below.

busy	good	big	convenient ✓
old	small	expensive	educated

EXAMPLE Wilson College is _more convenient than_ Jackson University for people with day jobs.

1. Jackson University is _____ Wilson College.

2. Classes at Wilson College are _____ classes at Jackson University.

3. Most students at Wilson College work full time. Students at Wilson
   College are _____ students at Jackson University.

4. Wilson College is _____ Jackson University
   for parents with small children.

5. Jackson University is _____ Wilson College.

6. Jackson University is _____ Wilson College.

7. Teachers at Jackson University are _____
   teachers at Wilson College.

EXERCISE 3 Fill in the blanks with the comparative form of the word in
parentheses ( ). Add *than* where necessary.

EXAMPLE **A:** I'm going to start my education at a community college.

B: Why?

A: It's ___*cheaper than*___ a four-year college.
            (cheap)

1. **A:** Which college do you prefer? Truman College or Northeastern

   University?

   B: I'm going to go to Truman College. It's _____ for
                                                    (convenient)

   me. It's _____ to my home and the tuition is less.
              (close)

   What about you?

   A: I'm going to study math. Northeastern has a good math program,

   so it's _____ for me.
            (good)

2. **A:** Are you going to buy new textbooks or used books?

   B: I prefer used books. They're _____ new books.
                                          (cheap)

   A: I prefer new books. They're _____. I don't like to
                                         (clean)

   see another student's answers in my book.

3. **A:** Some of the students in my class are married with children and

have full-time jobs. They're much _____ I am.
(busy)

B: You're only 18. You live with your parents, so going to college is

much _____ for you.
(easy)

4. **A:** I'm going to the bookstore to buy my books.

B: I'm going to buy my books online. Books in the bookstore are

_____ books online.
(expensive)

A: But it's _____ to get your books at the bookstore.
(fast)

B: You're right. It's _____ to get books from an online
(slow)

bookstore. But it only takes four or five days.

5. **A:** What are your plans for your education?

B: I'm going to get my general education at the community college.

Tuition is _____ there. Then I'm going to go to a
(cheap)

four-year college. But I'm going to feel a little strange there.

A: Why?

B: Because I'm 34 years old. I'm _____ most of the
(old)

other students.

6. **A:** My math teacher, Ms. Woods, is never in her office. Next

semester I'm going to take Mr. Riley's math class.

B: Why?

A: He's much _____ Ms. Woods.
(available)

7. **A:** My grades this semester are _____ my grades last
(bad)

semester.

B: Why?

A: I'm much _____ now. I have 12 credit hours
(busy)

and a full-time job. And my classes are much _____.
(hard)

EXERCISE **4** ABOUT YOU Compare yourself to your best friend.

EXAMPLE tall *I am taller than my best friend.*

1. responsible _____
2. educated _____
3. busy _____
4. funny _____
5. friendly _____
6. polite _____
7. tall _____
8. strong _____

10.3 | Comparisons with Nouns and Verbs

Examples	Explanation
Part-time students need **more time** to finish college.	We can use *more* before nouns to make a comparison statement.
You spend **less money** at a community college. My math class has **fewer students** than my biology class.	We can use *less* or *fewer* with nouns to make a comparison. Use *less* with noncount nouns. Use *fewer* with count nouns.
I prefer the city college because it costs **less.** You pay much **more** at a university. I study **harder** on the weekends.	We can use a comparative form after verbs.

EXERCISE **5** ABOUT YOU Find a partner and get information from him/her. Write sentences about you and your partner with the words given. Read your sentences to the class.

EXAMPLE have books *I have more books than Max.*

1. work hard _____
2. take classes _____
3. drive _____
4. have time to relax _____
5. study _____
6. have brothers and sisters _____

Compare Wilson College and Jackson University using the information below. The numbers in the table go with the numbers in the exercise.

	Wilson College	Jackson University
Example: number of students	2,000	10,000
1. cost per credit hour	$50	$145
2. night classes	150	50
3. books in library	8,000	50,000
4. number of campuses	5	2
5. number of students in a class	30	16
6. students over the age of 40	215	77
7. married students	800	200

EXAMPLE   Jackson University has _____*more students*_____ than Wilson College.

1. Wilson College costs _____ per credit hour.

2. Wilson College has _____ than Jackson University.

3. Wilson College has _____ in its library.

4. Wilson College has _____ than Jackson University.

5. Wilson College has _____ in a class.

6. Wilson College has _____ over the age of 40.

7. Jackson University has _____ than Wilson College.

EXERCISE 7 Shafia is in college. She is comparing herself to Simon's daughter, Tina. Tina is in high school. Fill in the blanks to complete this story.

Tina is in high school, and I'm in college. I have _____*more*_____
(example)

responsibilities than she does. Tina doesn't have to work, but I do. I

have a part-time job, and I'm taking 12 credit hours. I have

_____ work but _____ time to study.
       _(1)_   _(2)_

College classes are _____ high school classes. Tina
                               _(3)_

studies only two hours a day. I study four hours a day. I have

much _____ homework than she does.
        _(4)_

The class size is different too. My classes are

_____ Tina's classes. Her classes have 25 students.
       _(5)_

Some of my classes at college have 200 students.

Students at my college are all ages. Many students in my class are

much _____ I am. Some of them are my parents' age.
        _(6)_

In high school, all the students are about the same age.

LESSON 2

GRAMMAR

Superlative Forms of Adjectives
Spelling of the *–est* Forms
Superlatives with Nouns and Verbs

CONTEXT

Choosing a Used Car

Before You Read

1. Do you have a car? Is it a new car or a used car? What kind of car is it?

2. In your opinion, what are the best cars?

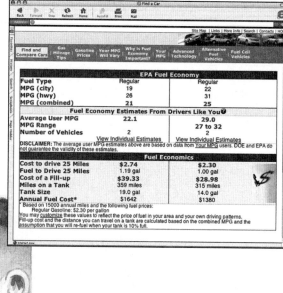

CHOOSING A USED CAR

Victor: I want to buy a used car. My co-worker, Sam, wants to sell me his 1999 car. He wants $4,000. Is that a good price?

Simon: I don't know. **The best** way to get information about used car prices is in the "blue book."

Victor: What's the "blue book"?

Simon: The "blue book" shows prices and other information about new and used cars. It can help you make a decision. We can look at it online.

After Simon goes online:

Simon: Look. Here's your co-worker's car.

Victor: There are three prices for the same car. Why?

Simon: The price depends on several things: condition of the car, mileage, and extras. Cars in **the best** condition with **the lowest** miles and the **most** extras are **the most expensive.** Cars with **the highest** mileage and **the most** problems are **the least expensive.**

Victor: Sam says his car is in good condition.

Simon: **The best** way to know for sure is to take it to a mechanic. You need a good car. Repairs are very expensive.

Victor: But it costs money to go to a mechanic.

Simon: It's better to lose $200 than $4,000. But the price of the car is not the only thing to consider. Also consider fuel economy. There's a Web site that compares fuel economy. Here it is. Look. Your co-worker's car gets only 22 miles per gallon (mpg). Look at these other two cars. This car gets 30 miles per gallon. This one gets 35 miles per gallon. Your co-worker's car is **the cheapest** to buy but it isn't **the most economical** to use.

Victor: There's a lot to know about buying a used car!

co-worker	Victor works with Sam. Sam is Victor's **co-worker.**
condition	My car is in good **condition.** I have no problems with it.
depends on	The price of the car **depends on** miles, condition, etc.
mileage	How many miles does the car have? What is its **mileage?**
consider	You have to **consider** a lot of things before you buy a car.
fuel economy/ economical	This car doesn't use a lot of gas. This car has good **fuel economy.** It is very **economical.**
extras	This car has a lot of **extras:** air-conditioning, a CD player, etc.
mechanic	A **mechanic** fixes cars.
repair	An old car needs a lot of **repairs.**
decision	There are many choices. He has to make a **decision.**

 **Did You Know?** When you buy a new or used car, you do not have to pay the asking price. The buyer can try to get a lower price from the seller.

🎧 **Listening Activity** Listen to the sentences about the conversation. Circle *true* or *false*.

EXAMPLE   TRUE   (FALSE)

1. TRUE   FALSE   5. TRUE   FALSE
2. TRUE   FALSE   6. TRUE   FALSE
3. TRUE   FALSE   7. TRUE   FALSE
4. TRUE   FALSE

10.4 | Superlative Forms of Adjectives

We use the superlative form to point out the number one item in a group of three or more. Add *the* before the superlative form.

Pattern	Simple Adjective	Comparative Adjective	Examples
Pattern 1: After a one-syllable adjective, add *-est*.	low tall	low**est** tall**est**	Car A has **the lowest** mileage.
Pattern 1 with a spelling change: After a two-syllable adjective that ends in *-y*, change *y* to *i* and add *-est*.	easy happy	eas**iest** happ**iest**	**The easiest** way to compare prices is with the "blue book."
Pattern 2: With other two-syllable adjectives and all three-syllable adjectives, add *the most* before the adjective.	helpful expensive	**the most** helpful **the most** expensive	Car A is **the most expensive** car.
Irregular Adjectives: We change the word completely.	good bad	**the best** **the worst**	Which car is in **the best** condition? Car C is in **the worst** condition.

Language Notes:

1. We often add a prepositional phrase after a superlative form.

   Your car is the oldest car **in the parking lot.**

2. You can use *one of the* with a superlative form. The noun it describes is plural.

   Lexus **is one of the** most expensive car**s.**

3. Omit *the* after a possessive form.

   My best friend has a 1995 Toyota.

Car A
28,000 miles
$11,000

Car B
75,000 miles
$4,000

Car C
150,000 miles
$700

10.5 | Spelling of -*est* Forms

Simple Adjective	Superlative Adjective	Explanation
old cheap	old**est** cheap**est**	Add -*est* to most adjectives.
big hot	big**gest** hot**test**	If the adjective ends with consonant-vowel-consonant, double the final consonant before adding -*est*.
nice late	nice**st** late**st**	If the adjective ends in *e*, add -*st* only.
busy easy	bus**iest** eas**iest**	If a two-syllable adjective ends in *y*, change *y* to *i* and add -*est*.

EXERCISE **1** Write the superlative form of the adjectives below. Use correct spelling.

1. convenient _____
2. big _____
3. fine _____
4. lazy _____
5. funny _____
6. expensive _____
7. friendly _____

8. hot _____
9. good _____
10. kind _____
11. mad _____
12. late _____
13. helpful _____
14. busy _____

EXERCISE **2** Victor is comparing three cars. Write superlative sentences about these three cars, using the information in the table and the words in parentheses ( ). The numbers in the table go with the numbers in the exercise.

Car A	Car B	Car C
Example: 28 mpg	25 mpg	20 mpg
1. big enough for 4 passengers	big enough for 5 passengers	big enough for 6 passengers
2. 1998	2004	2001
3. $4,000	$8,000	$10,000
4. needs work	in very good condition	in average condition

EXAMPLE   Car A is <u>*the most economical*</u>.
                          (economical)

1. Car C is _____ inside.
                (big)

2. Car A is _____. Car B is _____.
                (old)   *(new)*

3. Car C is _____. Car A is _____.
                (expensive)   *(cheap)*

4. Car B is in _____ condition. Car A is in
                    (good)

   _____ condition.
        (bad)

EXERCISE 3   Fill in the blanks with the superlative form.

1. *on the phone*

Shafia: I need your help. I want to buy a car. This is one of <u>*the biggest*</u>
                                                                    (big)

decisions of my life. What's _____ car?
                                    (good)

Dorota: I can't answer that question. It depends on your needs.

2. *at home*

Marta: You're going to graduate from high school next year. Let's talk
            about college for you. I prefer the city college for you because
            it's _____ to our home. It's also _____.
                    (close)   *(economical)*

Tina: I want to go to _____ college in the U.S. I want
                                (good)

to be a doctor.

Marta: You are choosing one of _____ professions.
                                            (hard)

Tina: I know, but I really want to be a doctor.

3. *at the bike shop*

Lisa: Let's choose a bike for you. This one looks good, but it's

_____.
    (heavy)

Maya: I don't like that one. I prefer this one. It's _____ of
                                                                (beautiful)

all the bikes.

4. *at the electronics store*

Halina: I need to buy a new computer. I want to buy _____ one.
(fast)

How about this one?

Peter: This one is probably _____.
(expensive)

5. *at the post office*

Halina: What's _____ way to send this package?
(economical)

Clerk: You can send it by third-class mail.

Halina: What's _____ way to send this package?
(fast)

Clerk: You can use express mail.

EXERCISE **4** ABOUT YOU Write about the number one person in your family for each of these items.

EXAMPLE tall *My brother Tim is the tallest person in our family.*

1. intelligent _____

2. beautiful _____

3. interesting _____

4. serious _____

5. funny _____

6. old _____

7. good cook _____

8. bad cook _____

10.6 | Superlatives with Nouns and Verbs

Examples	Explanation
Which car uses **the most gas**?	We can use *the most* before nouns to make superlative statements.
I want to spend **the least money** possible. This car has **the fewest** extras.	We can use *the least* and *the fewest* before nouns. Use *the least* with noncount nouns. Use *the fewest* with count nouns.
Which car costs **the most**? Who drives **the best** in your family?	We can use a superlative form after verbs.

EXERCISE 5 Victor and Simon are looking at car prices online. Fill in the blanks with the superlative form of the words in parentheses ( ).

Victor: Look at these ten cars. Maybe I should get _the cheapest_ car.
(example: cheap)

Simon: _____ is sometimes _____.
(1. cheap) *(2. expensive)*

Victor: How is that possible?

Simon: The cheapest car sometimes needs _____.
(3. repairs)

You should also consider fuel economy. This car gets 35 miles

per gallon. It's _____.
(4. economical)

Victor: But I like this one _____.
(5. good)

Simon: That one gets only 22 miles per gallon.

Victor: But it has _____: air-conditioning, power
(6. extras)

windows, sunroof, and more.

Simon: You want my advice, right? This is _____ advice
(7. good)

I can give you.

EXERCISE 6 ABOUT YOU Form a group with three classmates. Discuss the answers to these questions. Report your answers to the class.

1. Who speaks the most languages?
2. Who's the youngest?
3. Who's the best student?
4. Who has the longest last name?
5. Who's the newest immigrant?
6. Who's the tallest?
7. Who's the shortest?
8. Who's wearing the most jewelry?

9. Who has the largest family?

10. Who lives the closest to the school?

11. Who's taking the most classes?

12. Who has the longest hair?

13. Who talks the most in class?

EXERCISE **7** *Combination Exercise* Fill in the blanks with the comparative or superlative form of the word in parentheses ( ). Add *than* or *the* where necessary.

1. Gas in Europe is _____ gas in the U.S.
   (expensive)

2. There are three kinds of gas. Premium gas is _____ .
   (expensive)

3. I'm going to buy a car. I want to get _____
   (good)

   price, so I'm going to compare a lot of cars.

4. Can you help me buy a used car? You have _____
   (experience)

   I do.

5. I have many choices. I'm thinking of buying _____
   (economical)

   car.

6. Which car should I buy? I want to get _____
   (good)

   car possible for $4,000.

7. Is a Japanese car _____ an American car?
   (good)

8. This car is _____ that car.
   (cheap)

9. I'm looking at three cars. This car is _____ of all
   (pretty)

   of them. And it is in _____ condition. It probably
   (good)

   needs _____ repairs.
   (few)

10. My new car is _____ my old car.
    (beautiful)

11. A car is _____ a bicycle.
    (convenient)

EDITING ADVICE

1. Don't use -er and *more* together.

   My new car is ~~more~~ better than my old car.

2. Don't use -est and *most* together.

   I want to buy the ~~most~~ cheapest car.

3. Use *than* before the second item of comparison.

   This car is more expensive ∧ that car.

than

4. Don't confuse *then* and *than*.

   My English class is easier ~~then~~ my math class.

than

5. Use *the* before a superlative form.

   Which is ∧ best college?

the

6. Don't use *more* in superlative statements.

   My brother is the ~~more~~ interesting person in my family.

most

EDITING QUIZ

Find the mistakes with the underlined words, and correct them. Not every sentence has a mistake. If the sentence is correct, write *C*.

EXAMPLES Which is the ~~most~~ fastest car in the world?

My new car is <u>bigger than</u> my old car. *C*

1. Of these four cars, which one is <u>the more economical</u>?

2. My car gets <u>more better</u> mileage than your car.

3. Max is <u>the most intelligent</u> student in this class.

4. The teacher speaks English <u>better</u> I do.

5. The blue car costs <u>more then</u> the green car.

6. Her son is <u>best</u> student in his class.

7. Community college students are <u>oldest than</u> university students.

8. What is your <u>most worst</u> subject in school?

9. Who is the <u>more intelligent</u> student in this class?

LEARNER'S LOG

1. What did you learn in this unit? Write three sentences in your notebook about each topic.
   - Community colleges and four-year universities
   - Buying a used car

2. Write three questions you still have about colleges or buying a used car.

EXPANSION ACTIVITIES

Writing Activities

1. In your notebook, write six or seven sentences about the pictures. Compare Shafia's and Halina's English classes. Compare the room, the desks, the teachers, the time of class, and the homework.

EXAMPLE *Shafia's class has fewer students than Halina's class.*

2. In your notebook, compare three classes you are taking (for example: math, grammar, and reading). Write six or seven superlative sentences about your classes. Write about: hours of class each week, price of books, how easy the classes are, your grades in the classes, the amount of homework, how many students are in the classes, and how important each class is for you.

EXAMPLE *My chemistry class has the most credit hours.*

Outside Activity

Compare your family car to another car in your neighborhood. Or compare the cars of two friends. Tell the class the names of the cars. Compare age, condition, price, comfort, and how much you like each car.

EXAMPLE   My car is older than my brother's car.

Internet Activities

1. Search the words *blue book* and *used car prices*. Find the prices of three used cars. Tell the class the names of the cars, the condition, and the prices.

2. Search the words *compare fuel economy*. Find two cars you like. Tell the class about them.

UNIT
11

GRAMMAR

The Past Tense of *Be*
Regular Verbs in the Simple Past Tense
Irregular Verbs in the Past Tense
Time Expressions with the Past Tense

CONTEXT

Getting a Job

LESSON 1

GRAMMAR

Affirmative and Negative Statements with *Be*
Expressions of Time in the Past
Yes/No Questions with *Be*
Information Questions with *Be*
Subject Questions with *Be*

CONTEXT

Applying for a Job in a Store

Before You Read

1. What jobs can people get in stores?
2. How do people look for jobs?

APPLYING FOR A JOB IN A STORE

Halina is talking to Dorota on the phone.

Halina: I **was** at Baker's Department Store today.

Dorota: **Were** there any good sales?

Halina: I **wasn't** there for the sales. I **was** there to apply for a job. Positions are available now for work during the holidays. A lot of people **were** there. They **weren't** happy. There **was** a long line to apply for jobs.

Dorota: **Were** there interviews today too?

Halina: There **were** no interviews. I **was** surprised. The application **was** on a computer.

Dorota: Many big stores have job applications on the computer now. Employers usually interview people later. How **were** the questions on the application? **Were** they hard to answer?

Halina: They **weren't** difficult at all. The first questions **were** about my job history and education. There **were** questions about references. You **were** one of my references, Dorota.

Dorota: You can use me as a reference anytime. What **were** some other questions?

Halina: There **were** some funny questions. One **was:** "Your job starts at 8:00. Where should you be at 8:00? A) In the parking lot, B) In the employees' check-in room, or C) In your department.

Dorota: That's interesting. What **was** your answer?

Halina: It **wasn't** A. Time is important here. It **was** C, of course.

Vocabulary in Context

apply for	I want to **apply for** a new job. I have to fill out an application.
position	There are jobs available at Baker's. What **position** do you want to apply for?
interview (v.) interview (n.)	People from the store are going to talk to me. They are going to **interview** me. The **interview** is tomorrow.
surprised	I am **surprised.** He doesn't work at Baker's anymore.
reference	Can I use you as my **reference?** Employers are going to call you. They're going to ask you questions about me.
as	He used his employer **as** a reference. She works **as** a cashier. He wants a job **as** a salesman.
employer employee	My **employer** has a big business. He hires new people each year. These people are his **employees.**
check in	I have to **check in** at 8 a.m. for work.

Almost all stores and small businesses have at least one interview with future employees. Professional jobs often have two and sometimes three interviews.

 **Listening Activity** Listen to the sentences about the conversation. Circle *true* or *false*.

EXAMPLE (TRUE)   FALSE

1. TRUE   FALSE   5. TRUE   FALSE
2. TRUE   FALSE   6. TRUE   FALSE
3. TRUE   FALSE   7. TRUE   FALSE
4. TRUE   FALSE

11.1 | Affirmative and Negative Statements with *Be*

Subject	*Be* (Affirmative)	Complement
I	was	on time for work.
An employee	was	late today.
We	were	references for Halina.
You	were	at home today.
All the employees	were	busy.
There	was	a problem at work.
There	were	two new employees.

Subject	*Be* (Negative)	Complement
I	wasn't	in the office.
Her office	wasn't	open.
We	weren't	busy last night.
You	weren't	on the phone.
The employees	weren't	late for work.
There	wasn't	enough time.
There	weren't	any calls for you.

EXERCISE 1 Fill in the blanks with the affirmative or negative form of *be* in the past. Use the ideas from the conversation.

EXAMPLE Halina ____was____ at Baker's Department Store today.

1. Halina's job application _____ on a computer.

2. Some of the questions _____ funny.

3. Dorota _____ at the store with Halina today.

4. The questions on the application _____ hard to answer.

5. Dorota _____ a reference for Halina.

6. There _____ questions about Halina's job history on the application.

7. Halina _____ at Baker's for a sale.

8. People _____ in line for jobs at Baker's today.

11.2 | Expressions of Time in the Past

Examples	Explanation
I was in Chicago two days **ago**.	We use *ago* with numbers of minutes, hours, days, weeks, months, or years. It means *before now*.
He wasn't at work **yesterday**.	Yesterday is the day before today.
We were there **last week**. They weren't with us **last night**.	We use *last* with the words *night, week, month*, and *year*. It means the night, week, month, or year before the present one.

EXERCISE 2 ABOUT YOU Make statements about you. Use the words given. Use the affirmative or negative form of *be* in the past.

EXAMPLE at home last night
I wasn't at home last night.

1. in this class yesterday

   _____

2. on a bus this morning

   _____

3. on time for class today

_____

4. an employee of a store last year

_____

5. an employer in my country

_____

6. in my country two years ago

_____

7. a teenager five years ago

_____

11.3 | *Yes/No* Questions with *Be*

Be	Subject	Complement	Short Answer
Was	I	on time today?	Yes, you were.
Was	the new employee	at work today?	No, she wasn't.
Were	you	on a bus today?	Yes, I was.
Were	the new employees	late today?	No, they weren't.
Was	there	an interview today?	Yes, there was.
Were	there	any jobs available?	No, there weren't.

EXERCISE 3 Write a *yes/no* question about each statement. Use the words in parentheses ( ). Answer with a short answer. Use the ideas in the conversation.

EXAMPLE Halina was at Baker's Department Store today. (at a job interview)
Was she at a job interview? No, she wasn't.
_____

1. Many people were at Baker's. (to apply for jobs)

_____

2. There were questions on Halina's application. (about her job history)

_____

3. The job application was on a computer. (easy to fill out)

_____

4. Halina was surprised. (about the positions at Baker's)

_____

5. Many people were in line. (for interviews)

_____

6. Dorota was helpful. (a reference for Halina)

_____

11.4 | Information Questions with *Be*

Question Word	*Be*	Subject	Complement/ Time Expression	Short Answer
Why	**was**	Dorota's name	on Halina's job application?	Because Dorota was a reference.
Where	**were**	you	today?	At Baker's.
Who	**was**	your last employer?		Baker's Department Store.
How	**was**	your job interview	last week?	It was great!
Why	**were**	there	a lot of people at Baker's?	To apply for holiday positions.

EXERCISE 4 Complete the short conversations. Ask an information question about each statement. The underlined words are the answers.

EXAMPLE A: I wasn't at work today.

B: *Where were you?* _____

A: I was at a job interview.

1. A: My employer was surprised.

   B: _____

   A: Because I was an hour early for work.

2. A: There were a lot of questions on the application.

   B: _____

   A: They were easy.

3. **A:** There was a new employee in the store yesterday.

   B: _____

   A: It was <u>a young woman</u>. I don't know her name.

4. **A:** They were out of town for the holidays.

   B: _____

   A: <u>In Florida</u>.

5. **A:** I was at Baker's several days ago.

   B: _____

   A: <u>On December 23</u>.

6. **A:** Many positions were available at Baker's.

   B: _____

   A: <u>Sales positions</u>.

11.5 | Subject Questions with *Be*

Question Word (Subject)	Be	Complement	Short Answer
How many employees	**were**	late today?	Only one.
Which employee	**was**	late?	The new employee.

EXERCISE 5 Complete the short conversations with information questions as subjects. Use *be* in the past.

EXAMPLE **A:** Some employees were at the office yesterday.

   B: Who _*was there*_ ?

1. **A:** Many questions were on the application.

   B: What kind of _____?

2. **A:** Some people were surprised.

   B: Who _____?

3. **A:** Positions were available in that company last month.

   B: How many _____?

4. **A:** Something was wrong with your application.

   B: What _____?

5. **A:** Some of the questions were funny.

   B: Which _____?

EXERCISE 6 Shafia is very interested in Halina's job application. She is asking a lot of questions. Fill in their conversation with an expression from the box below. Use two of the expressions twice.

| there were | were | was | what was |
| were there | weren't | wasn't | were you ✓ |

Shafia: So, your application was on a computer. _Were you_
(example)

comfortable with that?

Halina: Sure. I know a lot about the computer. The computer was an

important part of my job in Poland.

Shafia: _____ your job in Poland?
(1)

Halina: I was in sales. Part of my job was to write sales reports.

Shafia: _____ a lot of questions about your job
(2)

history? American employers are very interested in that.

Halina: No. I have a very short job history.

Shafia: _____ it difficult to find references? I worry
(3)

about that. I don't know many people here.

Halina: Dorota was one reference for me. The other two

_____ friends of Peter's. It
(4)

_____ difficult to find references. People are
(5)

happy to be a reference for you.

Shafia: _____ any questions about American work
(6)

customs? Those are difficult. I don't know much about work
customs here.

Halina: _____ some questions. But they
(7)

_____ difficult to answer. There were three
(8)

possible answers. It _____ easy to choose
(9)

the correct answer most of the time.

LESSON 2

GRAMMAR

Affirmative Forms of Regular Past Tense Verbs
Spelling of the Regular *-ed* Form
Irregular Forms of the Simple Past Tense
Negative Forms of Regular and Irregular Past Tense Verbs

CONTEXT

Applying for a Job in an Office

Before You Read

1. Do you want a job in an office? Why or why not?

2. Where do you want to work? Why?

APPLYING FOR A JOB IN AN OFFICE

Halina and Dorota are talking about another job application.

Halina: I **had** a job interview today.

Dorota: Great! Was it at Baker's Department Store?

Halina: No. I **applied** for a job in an office. I **saw** an ad online for a sales position a few weeks ago. I **sent** my résumé. And they **called** me yesterday. I **went** for the interview this morning.

Dorota: That was fast. How was the interview?

Halina: Well, **I didn't get** there on time. I **didn't find** parking close to the office building. I **had to park** three blocks away.

Dorota: How late were you?

Halina: Only 15 minutes.

Dorota: Next time, go to the building the day before the interview. You can check travel time and parking then.

Halina: I **didn't like** the interview, Dorota. It **took** an hour. There were two people. They **asked** me a lot of questions. And I was nervous.

Dorota: What were some of the questions?

Halina: Well, one question was, "Why do you want this job?" I told them my last job was too hard. I **worked** long hours. I **didn't make** enough money.

Dorota: You shouldn't complain about your past jobs. Instead, say positive things about this new company.

Halina: I **did.** I **told** them some good things. Their company isn't too far from my neighborhood. It's easy to get there. I **didn't complain** about the parking.

Dorota: But you **didn't say** anything about the company. Find some information on the company's Web site. What does the company do? What do you like about it? It's important to know something about the company.

Halina: I **made** a lot of mistakes in this interview. I **said** the wrong things.

Dorota: Don't worry. It was good practice. The next time is going to be easier.

résumé	My **résumé** is very important. It has my job history and my education history on it.
ad	There are **ads** for jobs in the newspaper and online.
block	There's an office building three **blocks** from my house.
instead	I don't want coffee. I want tea **instead**.
positive	Don't complain. Say something **positive** instead.
make mistakes	Some of her answers on the test were wrong. She **made mistakes**.

Did You Know? Sometimes companies hire people for 90 day trial periods. If the employee does good work, he or she usually gets the job permanently after the 90 days.

Listening Activity

Listen to the sentences about the conversation. Circle *true* or *false*.

EXAMPLE (TRUE) FALSE

1. TRUE   FALSE
2. TRUE   FALSE
3. TRUE   FALSE
4. TRUE   FALSE

5. TRUE   FALSE
6. TRUE   FALSE
7. TRUE   FALSE

11.6 | Affirmative Forms of Regular Past Tense Verbs

We add *-ed* to the base form of the verb to form the past tense of many verbs. We use the past tense with actions completed in the past.

Subject	Verb + -ed	Complement
I	**complained**	about my last job.
He	**filled out**	the application.
Halina	**needed**	a job application.
We	**parked**	close to our work.
You	**wanted**	a better job.
The employers	**asked**	me a lot of questions.

Pronunciation Note: The affirmative ending *-ed* has three sounds: /d/, /t/, and /ɪd/. We pronounce the /ɪd/ sound if the verb ends in a *t* or *d* sound. Listen to your teacher pronounce the following sentences:

/d/ He played football.
      We used a computer.

/t/ She washed the dishes.
      You cooked the meal.

/ɪd/ They wan**t**ed a new car.
        I deci**d**ed to get a job.

EXERCISE **1** Fill in the blanks with the past tense of the verb in parentheses ( ). Use the ideas in the conversation.

EXAMPLE   Halina ____*parked*____ far from the office building.
                        (park)

1. Halina _____ an application for a sales job.
            (fill out)

2. A sales company _____ Halina for an interview.
                        (call)

3. Two people _____ Halina.
                (interview)

4. The people _____ Halina about her job history.
                (ask)

5. Halina _____ about her old job.
            (complain)

6. Dorota and Halina _____ about the interview.
                        (talk)

7. Halina _____ to say something positive
            (need)

about the new company during her interview.

11.7 | Spelling of the Regular *-ed* Form

Examples	Explanation
work/worked We **worked** there for three years.	For most verbs, add *-ed* to the base form.
live/lived She **lived** near her new work place.	If the verb ends in *e*, add *-d* only.
study/studied She **studied** for many years to get this job.	If the verb ends in consonant + *y*, change *y* to *i* and add *-ed*.
play/played The team **played** well.	If the verb ends in a vowel + *y*, do not change the *y* to *i*.

shop/shopped
 	
  s h o p
     ↓ ↓ ↓
     C V C
 	
She **shopped** for food yesterday.
	Double the final consonant if a single syllable word ends in consonant (C) + vowel (V) + consonant (C).

EXERCISE 2 Fill in the blanks with the past tense of the verb in parentheses ( ). Use the spelling rules from chart 11.7.

EXAMPLE   I ___*liked*___ my job in that company.
(like)

1. Many people _____ for the sales job.
(apply)

2. Employees in that company probably _____ for a long time.
(study)

3. You _____ in front of the office building.
(stop)

4. Those women _____ to work on Saturday.
(plan)

5. We _____ at the interview for half an hour.
(stay)

6. The company _____ some new workers for the holidays.
(hire)

11.8 | Irregular Forms of the Simple Past Tense

Base Form	Past Form	Base Form	Past Form	Base Form	Past Form
take	**took**	say	**said**	send	**sent**
have	**had**	tell	**told**	go	**went**
get	**got**	make	**made**	see	**saw**
know	**knew**	give	**gave**	do	**did**

Language Notes:
1. We use irregular past tense forms in the affirmative only.
2. Look for a complete list of irregular past tense forms in Appendix D.

EXERCISE 3 Fill in the blanks with the past tense of a verb from the box below. Use chart 11.8 to check for irregular past tense forms.

see ✓	have	send	give
go	get	tell	take

EXAMPLE   Halina ___*saw*___ two people at her interview.

1. Halina _____ a job interview last week.

2. She _____ her résumé to a company.

3. She _____ to the office building for an interview.

4. The interview _____ an hour.

5. Halina _____ information about the job online.

6. Dorota _____ Halina how to find information about the company.

7. Dorota _____ Halina some good advice.

11.9 | Negative Forms of Regular and Irregular Past Tense Verbs

We use *didn't* + the base form for the negative of both regular and irregular verbs in the past.

Subject	Didn't	Verb (Base Form)	Complement
I	**didn't**	work	at Baker's last year.
Halina	**didn't**	arrive	on time.
My employer	**didn't**	hire	any new employees.
You	**didn't**	apply	for the job.
We	**didn't**	know	all the answers.
They	**didn't**	give	the right answer.
Those ads	**didn't**	tell	the truth.

Language Note: Compare the affirmative and the negative.
  She **worked** on Saturday. She **didn't work** on Sunday.
  They **went** by car. They **didn't go** by bus.

EXERCISE 4 Use the words in parentheses ( ) to make a negative statement about the sentence given.

EXAMPLE Halina said many things. (positive things about the company)
But *she didn't say positive things about the company.*

1. Halina parked her car. (close to the office building)

   But _____

2. Halina interviewed for an office job. (at Baker's)

   But _____

3. Dorota went with Halina to the supermarket. (to her job interview)

   But _____

4. The new employees worked during the week. (on weekends)

   But _____

5. Halina used Dorota as a reference on her application. (Simon)

   But _____

EXERCISE 5   Complete the short conversations with the affirmative or negative past tense of the verb in parentheses ( ).

EXAMPLES   **A:** I used you as a reference on a job application.

     B: Yes, I know. The company ____*called*____ me yesterday.
                                                (call)

     A: I used you as a reference on a job application.

     B: I'm surprised. The company ____*didn't call*____ me.
                                                  (call)

1. **A:** Halina applied for a job at Baker's last month.

     B: Yes, but she _____ the job. She's looking for another
                              (get)

     job now.

2. **A:** You look nervous. What's wrong?

     B: I _____ a big mistake at work today.
               (make)

3. **A:** You didn't apply for the sales position. Why?

     B: I _____ time. I'm going to apply next week.
               (have)

4. **A:** I was surprised by the news.

     B: We were all surprised. We _____ this news.
                         (expect)

5. **A:** I don't work at that company now.

     B: Why? It's a good company.

     A: Yes. But they _____ me out of town on business
                        (send)

     too often. I _____ my family enough.
                    (see)

6. **A:** You have a new job now.

     B: Yes. How do you know?

     A: Your friend, Jesse, _____ me.
                    (tell)

EXERCISE 6 ABOUT YOU Use the words given to tell about your activities.
Use an affirmative or negative past tense sentence.

EXAMPLE stay home all day yesterday
I didn't stay home all day yesterday. OR I stayed home all day yesterday.

1. apply for a new job last week

2. use a computer yesterday

3. give the teacher my homework today

4. make a lot of mistakes on the last test

5. take a bus to school today

6. shop at a supermarket last week

7. talk to my teacher before class

EXERCISE 7 Complete the conversation between Dorota and Halina about
another job interview three weeks later. Use the affirmative or
negative past tense of the verb in parentheses ( ).

Halina: Thanks for your advice about interviews, Dorota. Unfortunately,

I ___*didn't get*___ the sales job. But I _____ another
(example: get)   (1. have)

interview this morning. It was for a position in another

company. The interview _____
(2. go)

very well this time.

Dorota: That's good.

Halina: I was on time. And I was prepared. I _____ about the
(3. learn)

company on the Web first. I _____ the interviewers
(4. tell)

positive things about their company. I _____ about
(5. complain)

my old job. I was lucky too. They _____ about Anna.
(6. ask)

I'm not sure about child care for her yet.

Dorota: Don't worry, Halina. They can't ask any personal questions
in a job interview. It's against the law.

Halina: Really? I _____ that.
(7. know)

GRAMMAR

Yes/No Questions in the Past—Regular and Irregular Verbs

More Irregular Verbs in the Past Tense

Information Questions in the Past

Subject Questions

CONTEXT

Jobs of the Future

Before You Read

1. Do you know some people with interesting jobs? What kind of jobs do they have?

2. In your opinion, what are the jobs of the future?

JOBS OF THE FUTURE

Matt is visiting Simon and Marta for the first time. Matt helped Marta's father in the hospital. Simon and Marta are talking about Matt's job.

Simon: So, Matt, you have an interesting career. You are a physical therapist, right?

Matt: Well, not exactly. I'm a PT assistant. I help the physical therapists in the hospital.

Marta: **Why did you choose** this career, Matt?

Matt: Well, I like physical activity. I like to help people. And a job in health services is a good job for the future. One in four new jobs is going to be in health services. **Did you know** that?

Simon: Yes. We read something about it last week.

Marta: **What did you do** to prepare for this job?

Matt: First, I took classes at a community college. I was in a special program for PT assistants.

Simon: **How long did it take?**

Matt: Two years. I got a certificate from the college.

Marta: **Did you have** on-the-job training also?

Matt: Yes. We had training at the hospital for some time. I worked with several physical therapists and their patients. I was so busy in those days. I had another job too.

Marta: **What did you do?**

Matt: I was a part-time fitness instructor at an athletic club. I thought about a career in fitness.

Simon: **How long did you stay** there?

Matt: Only a year. Two jobs took too much time.

Vocabulary in Context		
career	One **career** of the future is health services. Another **career** of the future is employment services.
patient	Marta's father was in the hospital. He was a **patient**.
physical therapist (PT)	A **physical therapist** helps patients move and exercise after an accident or injury.
training	Companies often give new employees on-the-job **training**. The employees learn about the job during **training**.
athletic club (health club)	People go to an **athletic club** to exercise. Sometimes we call it a health club.
fitness instructor	A **fitness instructor** works at a health club. He or she helps people with exercise and exercise machines.
temporary	His job is **temporary**. He is going to work for only four months.

Did You Know? Part-time or temporary work is a good way to find a job. Many people get their full-time job that way.

🎧 **Listening Activity** Listen to the sentences about the conversation. Circle *true* or *false*.

EXAMPLE TRUE ⬭FALSE⬭

1. TRUE FALSE
2. TRUE FALSE
3. TRUE FALSE
4. TRUE FALSE

5. TRUE FALSE
6. TRUE FALSE
7. TRUE FALSE

11.10 | *Yes/No* Questions in the Past—Regular and Irregular Verbs

The question pattern for regular and irregular verbs is the same. We use *did* + the base form.

Did	Subject	Verb (Base Form)	Complement	Short Answer
Did	I	**make**	a mistake?	Yes, you did.
Did	Matt	**choose**	a job in a health club?	No, he didn't.
Did	she	**get**	the job?	No, she didn't.
Did	we	**do**	the right thing?	Yes, you did.
Did	you	**have**	an interview?	No, I didn't.
Did	they	**stay**	with that company?	Yes, they did.

Language Note:

1. In normal speech, we pronounce *did you* as /dɪdʒə/, and *did he* as /dɪdi/. Listen to your teacher pronounce the following sentences:

   Did you see that man? Did he get the job?

   Did you know that? Did he have any training?

2. Compare the affirmative and question forms.

   He **worked** on Saturday. **Did** he **work** on Sunday?

   She **got** the job. **Did** she **get** a good salary?

EXERCISE 1 Write *yes/no* questions with the words given. Answer them with a short answer. Use the ideas in the conversation.

EXAMPLE Matt / need / an education for his job

Did Matt need an education for his job? Yes, he did.

1. Matt / study / at a university

   _____

2. Matt / choose / a good career for the future

   _____

3. Matt / help / Marta's father in the hospital

   _____

4. Simon and Marta / ask Matt a lot of questions

   _____

11.11 | More Irregular Verbs in the Past Tense

Base Form	Past Form	Base Form	Past Form	Base Form	Past Form
eat	**ate**	spend	**spent**	come	**came**
choose	**chose**	keep	**kept**	meet	**met**
read	**read***	feel	**felt**	leave	**left**
write	**wrote**	think	**thought**	hear	**heard**

***Pronunciation Note:** The past tense of **read** sounds like the color **red.**

EXERCISE 2 Fill in the blanks about the conversation with affirmative past tense verbs. Choose from the verbs above.

EXAMPLE Matt ___*spent*___ two years at a community college.

1. Marta _____ Matt in the hospital.

2. Matt _____ to visit Simon and Marta.

3. Matt _____ a career in health services.

4. Matt _____ about a career as a fitness instructor.

5. Simon _____ about careers in health services last week.

6. Matt _____ his job at the athletic club.

11.12 | Information Questions in the Past

Question Word	Did	Subject	Verb (Base Form)	Complement	Short Answer
Why	**did**	I	**get**	that job?	Because you had a lot of training.
What kind of job	**did**	Matt	**find?**		A job as a PT assistant.
Where	**did**	you	**go**	to school?	I went to a community college.
How many jobs	**did**	he	**apply for?**		Five.
How long	**did**	they	**work**	at their last job?	For five years.

EXERCISE 3   Write an information question for each answer in the short conversation. The underlined words are the answers.

EXAMPLE   **A:** _How many jobs did he apply for?_

B: He applied for three jobs.

1. **A:** _____

   B: I took classes at a community college.

2. **A:** _____

   B: She felt sick yesterday at work.

3. **A:** _____

   B: Matt knew four PT assistants in that hospital.

4. **A:** _____

   B: They heard about the job from friends.

5. **A:** _____

   B: Marta's father stayed in the hospital for three weeks.

6. **A:** _____

   B: Matt got a part-time job as a fitness instructor.

7. **A:** _____

   B: Matt chose a career as a PT assistant.

11.13 | Subject Questions

Use the verb in the past form with a subject question.

Question Word (Subject)	Verb -ed or Irregular Form	Complement	Short Answer
Which patient	**needed**	the doctor?	The woman in room 321.
How many patients	**came**	to the hospital?	Only one.
Who	**wrote**	about health careers?	A doctor.
What	**happened**	to her?	She got sick.

EXERCISE 4 Make questions with the words given. Use the question word as the subject. Use regular and irregular past tense verbs.

EXAMPLE Who / take / those people to the hospital

Who took those people to the hospital?

1. What / happen / at the health club yesterday

2. Who / tell / you about that job

3. How many people / apply for / the job as a fitness instructor

4. Which patient / spend / two weeks at the hospital

5. Which student / choose / a job in health services

11.14 | More Irregular Verbs in the Past Tense

Base Form	Past Form	Base Form	Past Form	Base Form	Past Form
put	**put***	fall	**fell**	pay	**paid**
break	**broke**	hurt	**hurt***	cost	**cost***
find	**found**	understand	**understood**	buy	**bought**
drive	**drove**	lose	**lost**	sell	**sold**
Language Note: *Some verbs use the base form as the irregular past.					

Write a question and an answer with the words given. Use the words in parentheses ( ) in the answer.

EXAMPLE Where / she / hurt her arm (at the health club)

Where did she hurt her arm?

She hurt it at the health club.

1. Which arm / she / break (her right arm)

   _____

   _____

2. How much / his classes / cost ($55 per credit hour)

   _____

   _____

3. What kind of books / she / buy for school (science books)

   _____

   _____

4. How / you / find that job (on the Internet)

   _____

   _____

5. When / they / lose their jobs (last week)

   _____

   _____

6. Who / fall (the patient)

   _____

   _____

7. Which college / he / choose (a community college)

   _____

   _____

8. How much / the students / pay for training (a lot of money)

   _____

   _____

9. Who / drive / her to the hospital (her husband)

   _____

   _____

EDITING ADVICE

1. Don't use the past tense after *to* (the infinitive).

            spend
   He wanted to ~~spent~~ all the money.

2. Use the base form after *did* and *didn't*.

           go
   Where did they ~~went~~ after class?

       find
   They didn't ~~found~~ the answer.

3. Don't use *did* in subject questions. Use the past form.

       happened
   What ~~did happen~~ at school today?

4. Remember to change the spelling of the *-ed* forms for certain verbs.

       applied
   She ~~applyed~~ to that school.

5. Don't forget to change irregular verbs to the correct past tense form.

       hurt   *broke*
   I ~~hurted~~ my leg.   He ~~breaked~~ his arm.

EDITING QUIZ

Find the mistakes with the underlined words, and correct them. Not every sentence has a mistake. If the sentence is correct, write *C*.

                                   arrive
EXAMPLES The employees didn't ~~arrived~~ on time.

             He <u>chose</u> a career in health services. *C*

1. Did they <u>had</u> an interview today?

2. He <u>keeped</u> that job for three years.

3. What <u>they said</u> to her?

4. Who <u>did make</u> a mistake?

5. We <u>felt</u> good after the interview.

6. She <u>didn't understood</u> the company rules.

7. They <u>tryed</u> to get a good job.

1. What did you learn in this unit? Write three sentences in your notebook about each topic:
    - applying for a job
    - a job interview
    - jobs of the future

2. Write three questions you still have about jobs in the United States.

EXPANSION ACTIVITIES

Writing Activity

In your notebook, rewrite the following conversation between Matt and a new patient, Tracy. Change *now* to *last year*. Make the necessary changes to the verbs.

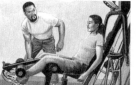

Tracy: Now I work in the employment services department at Baker's Department Store.

Matt: What do you do there?

Tracy: I keep information about employees. I help employees with their taxes and health insurance. And I write reports.

Matt: How do you get a job like that?

Tracy: Well, it isn't difficult. It takes two years to get a certificate in business.

Matt: Do you like your job?

Tracy: No, I don't. I don't want to work in business. I want a career in health services like you.

Outside Activities

1. Find a health or exercise club in your city or town. Call or visit it. Ask how much it costs to be a member. Ask about the activities at the club. Tell the class about the club.

2. Go to a store near you. Ask for a job application and fill it out for practice.

Internet Activity

Search the words *Occupational Outlook Handbook*. Look for an interesting job. Find it in the handbook. Find the answers to these questions about the job. Tell the class about the job.
    - What education is necessary?
    - What is the average pay for this job?
    - Are jobs like this growing faster than average?

UNIT

12

GRAMMAR

Verb Review: Simple Present Tense
Present Continuous Tense
Future Tense
Simple Past Tense
Modal Verbs: *Can, Should, Must, Have To*

CONTEXT

Giving Back

LESSON 1

GRAMMAR

Review of Verb Tenses—Affirmative and Negative
Review of Infinitives
Review of Modal Verbs—Affirmative and Negative
Review of Time Expressions

CONTEXT

Helping Others

Before You Read

1. What help did you need as a newcomer?

2. What do you do to help other newcomers?

HELPING OTHERS

Simon, Dorota, Victor, Lisa, and Halina are in a coffee shop.

Victor: Simon, thanks for your help on moving day. With your help, it **didn't take** us so long. You **gave** me some good advice about used cars too. But I **don't have** a car yet. **I'm** still **looking.**

Simon: How is your new apartment?

Lisa: We **are** very comfortable there. It's big and sunny. Our daughter **likes** her new school too. She **doesn't have to walk** far. We**'re all enjoying** life in the U.S. now. We **don't feel** like newcomers anymore. Thanks for all your help.

Simon: No problem. Any time.

Halina: I **want to thank** you, Dorota. With your help, I **learned** about many important places in this city. Also, you **helped** me with my Social Security card. And your advice about job interviews **was** very helpful. I really **like** my new job. I**'m going to stay** with this company for a while.

Dorota: I **was** happy to help, Halina.

Halina: My life **is** easier now. I **don't feel** so confused. Maybe I **can help** you in your work with newcomers. I **can be** a volunteer. I**'m not going to be** so busy from now on.

Victor: You **can count on** my help too.

Simon: That's good. Marta and I **are going to have** a meeting for volunteers next week. You **should come.** It **isn't going to take** a long time. And you **can learn** about other volunteer activities too. There are many opportunities to help others.

volunteer (n.) volunteer (v.)	I'm a **volunteer** for newcomers. I also **volunteer** at a day care center. They do not pay me for my work.
newcomer	My friend just arrived in the U.S. He is a **newcomer.**
really + verb	He **really needed** a new TV. It was very important to get a new TV. His old TV broke.
from now on	This is my last day to take the bus to work. **From now on,** I'm going to drive.
opportunity	I have an **opportunity** to work at Baker's Department Store. I can work there if I want to.
count on	We can help you. We are available all day Saturday. You can **count on** us to help you on Saturday.

The number of American volunteers goes up every year. Between 60 and 65 million Americans volunteer each year. They volunteer at least one hour a week.

12.1 | Review of Verb Tenses—Affirmative and Negative

The Simple Present Tense

	Examples	Explanation
Be	a. Dorota **is** 40 years old. b. Victor **isn't** a volunteer yet. c. Dorota **is** from Poland. d. Simon and Marta **aren't** Polish. e. The five friends **are** in a coffee shop. f. It **isn't** cold today. g. It **is** 3:00 p.m. h. Halina and Victor **are** happy. Their lives **aren't** as difficult now.	a. Age b. Occupation/work c. Place of origin d. Nationality e. Location f. Weather g. Time h. Description
There + Be	a. **There is** a need for volunteers. b. **There aren't** many newcomers here today.	Use *there is* and *there are* to talk about a subject for the first time.
Other Verbs	a. Halina **works** in an office. b. Dorota **doesn't work** every day.	a. Facts b. Habits, customs, regular activity

The Present Continuous Tense

Examples	Explanation
a. Halina **is thanking** Dorota. b. Halina **isn't looking** for a job at this time.	a. Actions at the present moment b. Actions at a present time period

The Future Tense with *Be Going To*

	Examples	Explanation
Be	Halina and Victor **are going to be** volunteers.	Future plans Predictions for the future
There + Be	**There isn't going to be** a volunteer meeting tomorrow.	
Other Verbs	Halina **is going to help** newcomers. Halina **is going to have** more free time soon.	

The Simple Past Tense

	Examples	Explanation
Be	Halina **was** a salesperson in Poland.	Actions completed in the past
There + Be	There **weren't** many people in the coffee shop yesterday.	
Regular Verbs	Victor **moved** to a new apartment two weeks ago. He **didn't move** far away.	
Irregular Verbs	Halina **didn't get** a job in a store. She **got** a job in an office.	

EXERCISE 1 Complete each sentence about the conversation with the correct tense of the verb in parentheses ( ). Use affirmative verbs.

EXAMPLE   Halina ___*is talking*___ to Dorota now.
           (talk)

1. Simon, Dorota, Halina, Lisa, and Victor _____ together
   (sit)

   in a coffee shop.

2. Victor's family _____ a bigger apartment.
   (find)

3. Victor _____ his new apartment.
   (like)

4. Victor and Halina _____ American life now.
   (enjoy)

5. Simon _____ Victor good advice about used cars.
   (give)

6. Victor _____ a used car soon.
   (buy)

7. Halina and Victor _____ newcomers several months ago.
   _(be)_

8. Halina _____ a Social Security card.
   (have)

9. Dorota _____ Halina get her Social Security card.
   (help)

10. Halina _____ Dorota with other newcomers from now on.
    (help)

EXERCISE 2   Read each sentence. Write the negative form with the words in parentheses ( ).

EXAMPLE   The five friends are having coffee now. (lunch)

They aren't having lunch. _____

1. Victor and Halina are talking about their lives now. (their problems)

   _____

2. Victor wanted to move. (stay in his old apartment)

   _____

3. His old apartment was too small. (big enough for his family)

   _____

4. Victor feels comfortable in America now. (strange anymore)

   _____

5. Simon gave Victor advice. (about jobs)

   _____

6. Halina and Victor had a lot to do at first. (much free time then)

   _____

7. Halina's life is easier now. (so difficult)

   _____

8. She is going to work in her company for a while. (look for another job soon)

   _____

12.2 | Review of Infinitives

Examples	Explanation
Halina started **to work** for a new company. She expects **to stay** there for a while. It's fun **to be** a volunteer. Halina wants **to be** a volunteer. Victor is trying **to buy** a used car.	• The infinitive is formed by *to* and the base form of the verb. • Infinitives can go after adjectives or verbs. • The tense is always in the verb before the infinitive.

EXERCISE 3   Complete each sentence with an infinitive expression.

EXAMPLE   It's good <u>*to help other people*</u>   .

1. Victor wants ————————————————.
2. Halina needed ————————————————.
3. Halina learned ————————————————.
4. It's not easy ————————————————.
5. Simon and Marta like ————————————————.
6. Simon and Marta are trying ————————————————.
7. Halina and Victor are expecting ————————————————.

12.3 | Review of Modal Verbs

Can, Should, Must, Have To

Examples	Explanation
a. Victor **can speak** English better now. b. He doesn't have his driver's license. He **can't drive** now. c. Victor and Halina **can volunteer** now.	a. Ability—no ability b. Permission—not permitted c. Possibility—impossibility
a. We **should help** other people. b. You **shouldn't arrive** late to an interview.	Advice, suggestion
a. Everyone **must get** a Social Security card in order to work. b. You **must not drive** without a driver's license.	a. Strong obligation from a rule or law b. Strong obligation not to do something because of a rule or law
a. Victor's daughter **has to go** to school. b. She **doesn't have to go** to a public school.	a. Strong necessity or obligation (by law, custom, rule, or personal necessity) b. Not necessary

EXERCISE 4 ABOUT YOU Fill in the blanks with the affirmative or negative form of the modals in parentheses ( ). Make sentences that are true about you.

EXAMPLES

<u>   I have to   </u> work tonight.
(have to)

<u> I don't have to </u> work on weekends.
(have to)

1. _____ speak English every day.
      (should)

2. _____ go to school.
      (have to)

3. _____ speak English like an American.
      (can)

4. _____ speak my language in this class.
      (should)

5. _____ drive without a license.
      (must)

6. _____ pay for classes at this school.
      (have to)

EXERCISE 5 Halina, Victor, Simon, and Dorota continue their conversation. Fill in the blanks with the correct forms of the verbs in parentheses ( ). Use the different tenses, infinitives, and modals.

Part 1: **Dorota:** There's a lot to do. Sometimes we _____ enough
(1. get, negative)
volunteers to help.

Victor: What else do volunteers do?

Simon: Well, many newcomers _____ how to drive. They
(2. know, negative)
_____ sure about the rules on American roads.
(3. be, negative)
Volunteers _____ people get their driver's
(4. can / help)
licenses. Tomorrow, Dorota and I _____ with a
(5. meet)
group of newcomers. One young man _____ to
(6. need / drive)
work every day. I _____ with him yesterday. But
(7. practice)
I _____ out of town next weekend.
(8. be)

Victor: I _____ him. But I _____ a car yet.
(9. want / help)   (10. have, negative)

Part 2: **Dorota:** Next Thanksgiving, we _____ a holiday dinner
(1. prepare)
for newcomers. We _____ volunteers now. It's
(2. look for)
difficult _____ people right before a holiday.
(3. find)
Everyone is so busy then.

Halina: Peter and I _____ you. I _____.
(4. want / help)   (5. can / cook)

Dorota: Thanks, Halina. My friend Nancy _____ with new-
(6. work)
comers from all over the world. She _____ holiday
(7. prepare)
meals every year at a school in her neighborhood. You can help.

12.4 | Review of Time Expressions

always	sometimes	this week	right away
never	hardly ever	in a few weeks	yesterday
from now on	rarely	next week	last year
often	right now	soon	two weeks ago
usually	at the moment	tomorrow	every week

EXERCISE 6 Circle the time expressions in the following sentences. Then fill in the blanks in the sentences with an affirmative verb from the box. Use the correct tense. Two verbs are used twice.

help	move	tell ✓	write	give	have
know	enjoy	come	teach	find	invite

EXAMPLE At the coffee shop (yesterday,) Dorota _____*told*_____ Halina about her friend, Nancy.

1. Nancy often _____ newcomers.

2. These newcomers hardly ever _____ all the items necessary for their new life in America.

3. Nancy _____ them clothes and household items.

4. The items usually _____ from Nancy's friends and co-workers and charities.

5. Last year five new families from Africa _____ into Nancy's neighborhood.

6. Nancy _____ them enough items for a comfortable home.

7. She _____ jobs for them too.

8. These families _____ their new life in America now.

9. These days, Nancy _____ these families about American life.

10. She _____ the newcomers to her famous Thanksgiving dinner later this year.

11. Last year after the dinner, a city newspaper _____ a story about Nancy's work with newcomers.

12. Now everyone _____ about Nancy's work.

13. She _____ many new volunteers to help her in the future.

EXERCISE 7 Look at the picture below. Write a paragraph about the picture. Use all the tenses you learned in this book: simple present, present continuous, future (*be going to*), simple past, and modal verbs. Use affirmative and negative sentences.

EXAMPLES Newcomers are going to have an American Thanksgiving dinner.

There's a turkey on each table. Volunteers prepared the turkey.

_____

_____

_____

_____

_____

_____

_____

_____

_____

_____

LESSON 2

GRAMMAR

Yes/No Questions
Review of Information Questions

CONTEXT

Volunteer Activities

Before You Read

1. What volunteer activities do you know about?
2. Why do people volunteer?

VOLUNTEER ACTIVITIES

At Marta's volunteer meeting.

Marta: Good evening, everyone. These are my friends Rhonda, Val, and Elsa. They are volunteers. They are going to give you information. They're going to answer your questions about volunteer work. Rhonda, **are you** ready? **What is your volunteer group doing** this month?

Rhonda: Hello, everyone. My name is Rhonda and I work for an airline. We have a program to help poor children in other countries. This month we are planning a trip to South America. We are going to bring wheelchairs, eyeglasses, and medical supplies to people in small villages.

Marta: **Who gives** you these supplies, Rhonda?

Rhonda: Many people know about our program. They collect old eyeglasses for us. Doctors give us medical supplies. Other charities help us too. And our airline pays for the flights.

Marta: **Do you bring** anything else to these people?

Rhonda: Yes. We bring clothing for children and adults, too. And we also have special projects each year.

Marta: **What did your group do** last year, Rhonda? **Was it** a special project?

Rhonda: Yes, it was. We brought a sick little boy from South America here to the U.S. He needed an operation. They didn't have medical care in his village. Two months later, I brought a healthy boy back to his parents. They were so happy. And I was too.

Marta: **How can we help? Do volunteers have to work** for the airline?

Rhonda: No. Anyone can give us these supplies.

Marta: **What are you going to do** next?

Rhonda: We are going to give gifts to the kids in one village at a special holiday party. Right now we are collecting children's clothing and toys.

Marta: **Does anyone have** a question for Rhonda?

Vocabulary in Context

fly (v.) flight (n.)	I'm going to **fly** from New York to Miami today. My **flight** leaves at 5 p.m.
airline	What **airline** are you taking to Miami?
wheelchair	Peter can't walk. He needs a **wheelchair.**
bring— brought	A: What did you **bring** to class today? B: I **brought** my book.
project	Rhonda's **project** is to collect clothing for newcomers to the U.S.
village	Only 500 people live in his **village.**
operation	Tom broke his leg. He needed an **operation** in the hospital.
collect	I **collect** old clocks. I have 20 of them now.

Most volunteers in America are women between the ages of 35 and 44. But volunteers over age 60 give the most hours of their time.

12.5 | *Yes/No* Questions

The Simple Present Tense

	Yes/No Questions	Short Answers
Be	**Is** she at home?	Yes, she is.
	Are the volunteers from South America?	No, they aren't.
There + Be	**Is there** a meeting at your house?	Yes, there is.
	Are there any volunteers at the meeting?	No, there aren't.
Other Verbs	**Does** Dorota **work** for an airline?	No, she doesn't.
	Do charities **help** the volunteers?	Yes, they do.

The Present Continuous

Yes/No Questions	Short Answers
Is Rhonda **talking** to the group?	Yes, she is.
Are you **learning** about volunteer activities?	No, I'm not.
Are the volunteers **asking** for money?	No, they aren't.

The Future with *Be Going To*

Yes/No Questions	Short Answers
Am I **going to need** help?	Yes, you are.
Is there going to be a meeting?	No, there isn't.
Are the people **going to ask** questions?	Yes, they are.

The Simple Past Tense

	Yes/No Questions	Short Answers
Be	**Were** you a volunteer last year? **Was** he in South America last week? **Were** the volunteers helpful last year?	No, I wasn't. Yes, he was. Yes, they were.
There + Be	**Was there** a problem with the volunteers last year? **Were there** enough volunteers to help people?	No, there wasn't. Yes, there were.
Regular and Irregular Verbs	**Did** Rhonda **help** someone? **Did** they **bring** toys to the children?	Yes, she did. No, they didn't.

Modal Verbs

	Yes/No Questions	Short Answers
Should	**Should** we volunteer for that project?	Yes, we should.
Can	**Can** I volunteer?	Yes, you can.
Have to	**Does** she **have to** volunteer today? **Do** doctors **have to** come to the meeting?	No, she doesn't. Yes, they do.

Language Note: Questions with *must* are not common. We use *have to* for questions.

EXERCISE 1 Ask a *yes/no* question about the conversation. Use the words given. Use the same tense as in the statement. Answer your question with a short answer.

EXAMPLE Rhonda has a job. (with an airline)

Does Rhonda have a job with an airline? Yes, she does.

1. Rhonda is talking. (about her job with the airline)

   _____

2. Rhonda brings medical supplies to poor children. (wheelchairs)

   _____

3. A little boy needed medical care last year. (an operation)

   _____

4. The sick boy was in a village. (in the United States)

_____

5. Rhonda brought the boy to the United States. (back to his parents)

_____

6. The volunteers are going to have a party. (in the United States)

_____

7. There are many people at Marta's house today. (any volunteers)

_____

8. People should give Rhonda toys for the holiday party. (medical supplies)

_____

9. People can ask Rhonda questions. (about other projects)

_____

12.6 | Review of Information Questions

Simple Present Tense		
	Information Questions	**Answers**
Be	Who **is** Rhonda? Where **are** Rhonda, Val, and Elsa?	She's a volunteer. They're at Marta's house.
There + Be	Why **is there** a meeting today at Marta's house? How many people **are there** at the meeting?	To give information about volunteer work. About 20.
Other Verbs: Questions about the Complement	Where **does** Rhonda **work?** How **do** doctors **help?**	With an airline. They give medical supplies.
Subject Questions	Who **collects** eyeglasses? Which airline **helps** people?	Many people. Rhonda's airline.

Present Continuous Tense

	Information Questions	Answers
Questions About the Complement	Who **is** Rhonda **talking** to? What **are** volunteers **collecting** now?	New volunteers. Children's clothing and toys.
Subject Questions	How many volunteers **are speaking** at the meeting?	Three.

Future Tense

	Information Questions	Answers
Be	What **is** the special project **going to be?** When **are you going to be** a volunteer?	A holiday party for kids. Next month.
There + Be	When **is there going to be** another meeting? How many meetings **are there going to be?**	Next week. Only two more.
Questions About the Complement	What **is** Rhonda **going to do** with the toys? When **are** the volunteers **going to give** the toys to the children?	She's going to give them to kids. In December.
Subject Questions	Which children **are going to get** the gifts? Who **is going to be** at the meeting?	The children in one small village. Many new volunteers.

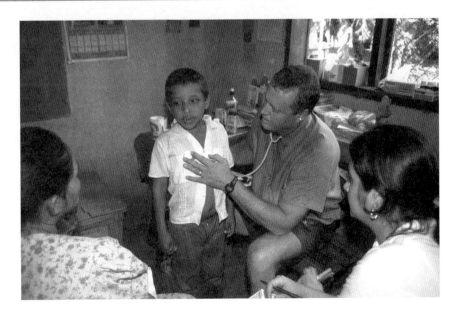

Simple Past Tense

	Information Questions	Answers
Be	Where **was** the meeting? Why **were** the parents worried?	We don't know. Because there was no medical care in the village.
There + Be	Why **was there** a special project last year? What kind of help **was there** for the boy?	Because a little boy was sick. Medical help.
Questions About the Complement: Regular and Irregular Verbs	What kind of help **did** the boy **need?** When **did** the boy **have** his operation?	He needed an operation. He had it last year.
Subject Questions	Which volunteers **brought** the boy to the U.S.?	The women from the airline.

Modal Verbs

	Information Questions	Answers
Questions About the Complement	When **can** we help Rhonda? How **should** we help her? When **does** Rhonda **have to** get the toys?	You can help right now. You can give her clothing and toys. A week before the holiday trip.
Subject Questions	Who **can** help Rhonda? How many children **had to get** help in that village last year?	All of us can help her. Two or three.
Language Note: Questions with *must* are not common. Use *have to* for questions.		

EXERCISE 2 Write an information question about each sentence. Use the question words in parentheses ( ).

EXAMPLE Rhonda has a job (What kind)

What kind of job does she have?

She works for an airline.

1. Rhonda does volunteer work. (What kind)

   _____

   _____

2. Rhonda went to South America last year. (Why)

   _____

   _____

3. Someone pays for the flights to South America. (Who)

   _____

   _____

4. The volunteers are going to have a party for children. (When)

   _____

   _____

5. A sick boy had to come to the U.S. (Why)

   _____

   _____

6. People should help with the holiday project. (How)

   _____

   _____

7. Rhonda is explaining something to the new volunteers. (What)

   _____

   _____

EXERCISE **3** Look at the picture below. Rhonda is at the special Christmas party for the children. Write six questions about the picture. Use *yes/no* questions and information questions. Use all the tenses: simple present, present continuous, future, past, and modal verbs. Write the short answers.

EXAMPLES *Is there a Christmas tree at the party.*

What is the little girl asking Santa?

1. _____
2. _____
3. _____
4. _____
5. _____
6. _____

EXERCISE **4** Val, a second volunteer at Marta's meeting, tells the group about her activities. People are asking her questions about her volunteer activities. Write their questions with the words given. Use the answer to help you with the tense.

EXAMPLE   Man: Where ___*do you volunteer*___?
                        (you / volunteer)

Val: I volunteer in my neighborhood. My volunteer job is very interesting. I also work with children. I work at a day care center for single moms. I work there once a week. There are other volunteers too. We help with the children. We also plan special projects.

1. Woman: How _____?
                    (the center / help single moms)

   Val: Mothers pay half the cost of regular day care centers.

2. Woman: How many _____ in the class?
                        (children / there)

   Val: Every day is different. There are usually about 15 or 20 kids.

3. Man: How many _____?
                    (hours / each volunteer / work)

   Val: Each volunteer works four hours on their day.

4. Man: What day _____ last week?
                    (you / work)

   Val: I worked on Thursday last week.

5. Woman: What _____?
                    (you / do)

   Val: I helped with the art activities, I served the meals, and I played with the children a lot.

6. Man: How _____ about this day care center?
                (you / find out)

   Val: It was on our city's Web site. That's a good place to look for volunteer opportunities.

7. Woman: What special project _____ now?
                            (the volunteers / plan)

   Val: We're planning an art show and sale of the children's art.

8. **Man:** What kind of art _____?
   (children / learn)

   Val: We're teaching them to paint.

9. **Man:** When _____?
   (the sale / be)

   Val: In three months. I can tell you the date later.

10. **Woman:** What _____ to help?
    (we / should do)

    Val: You should come to the sale. The money is for the kids.

11. **Man:** What _____ with the money?
    (center / do)

    Val: We are going to buy books for the new children's library.

EXERCISE 5   Elsa is talking now. People are asking Elsa questions. Complete each question with the words given. Use the answers to help you with the tense.

Marta: This is Elsa. She volunteers to help older people. She works with a neighborhood group. She works one week each month.

Woman: _____Are you going to work_____ this week, Elsa?
  (example: you / work)

Elsa: Yes, I am. I'm going to help an older woman in my neighborhood. She can't see very well and she lives alone.

Man: How _____?
  (1. you / help her)

Elsa: I'm going to take her to a doctor's appointment tomorrow, and I'm going to get her groceries on the weekend.

Woman: What _____ all day?
  (2. this woman / do)

Elsa: She goes to the gym two days a week. A volunteer takes her. She exercises in a swimming pool.

Woman: _____?
  (3. she / can swim)

Elsa: She doesn't exactly swim. She takes a special class for seniors. It's exercise in the water.

Woman: When _____ these classes?
  (4. she / start)

Elsa: She started the classes 20 years ago. She says, "This class is responsible for my long life." Last week she turned 90.

EDITING ADVICE

1. Always use the base form after *doesn't*, *don't*, *didn't*, *to*, and modals.

   go
   They didn't ~~went~~ to the meeting today.

   fix
   He wanted to ~~fixed~~ the car for her.

   He should ~~to~~ go to work on time.

2. Don't use a form of *be* with the simple present or past tenses.

   went
   I ~~am~~ go to the store every week. She ~~was~~ go to the store yesterday.

3. Don't use *do*, *does*, or *did* in a subject question.

   works
   Who ~~does work~~ as a volunteer?

4. Don't forget to use *do*, *does*, or *did* in a question about the complement.

   did he work
   Where ~~he worked~~?

5. Use the correct word order in questions.

   is he
   When ~~he is~~ going to drive her to the supermarket?

EDITING QUIZ

Find the mistakes with the underlined words, and correct them. Not every sentence has a mistake. If the sentence is correct, write *C*.

EXAMPLES   She should <u>helps</u> Marta.
Where did <u>you go</u>?   *C*

1. Does that <u>volunteer has</u> a full-time job?

2. Why <u>I should</u> volunteer?

3. She <u>have to worked</u> extra hours last week.

4. Marta <u>didn't invited</u> too many people to her house.

5. They <u>shouldn't to complain</u> about their job.

6. How many volunteers <u>did worked</u> at the day care center last week?

7. Val <u>can count</u> on the new volunteers.

1. Write three sentences in your notebook about each topic. Use a different tense in each sentence.
   - Val's volunteer job
   - Elsa's volunteer job
   - Rhonda's volunteer job

2. Write three questions you still have about volunteers.

EXPANSION ACTIVITIES

Writing Activity

In your notebook, write five to six true sentences about the picture. Write at least one sentence with each tense you learned in this book: the present continuous, simple present, future, past, and a modal verb.

Outside Activity

Ask some Americans about their volunteer work. What do they do? How often? Tell the class what you learned.

Internet Activities

1. Search the words *volunteer opportunities* and the name of your city. Find an interesting volunteer activity. Tell the class about it.

2. Go to the Web site: *www.usafreedomcorps.gov*. This site offers volunteer jobs for the U.S. government. Find an interesting volunteer opportunity and tell the class about it.

Appendices

The Calendar

Months	Days	Seasons
January (Jan.)	Sunday (Sun.)	Winter
February (Feb.)	Monday (Mon.)	Spring
March (Mar.)	Tuesday (Tues.)	Summer
April (Apr.)	Wednesday (Wed.)	Fall or Autumn
May	Thursday (Thurs.)	
June (Jun.)	Friday (Fri.)	
July (Jul.)	Saturday (Sat.)	
August (Aug.)		
September (Sept.)		
October (Oct.)		
November (Nov.)		
December (Dec.)		

Dates

January 6, 1999 or Jan. 6, 1999 or 1/6/99 or 1-6-99

October 27, 2004 or Oct. 27, 2004 or 10/27/04 or 10-27-04

Numbers

Cardinal Numbers	Ordinal Numbers
1 = one	first
2 = two	second
3 = three	third
4 = four	fourth
5 = five	fifth
6 = six	sixth
7 = seven	seventh
8 = eight	eighth
9 = nine	ninth
10 = ten	tenth
11 = eleven	eleventh
12 = twelve	twelfth
13 = thirteen	thirteenth
14 = fourteen	fourteenth
15 = fifteen	fifteenth
16 = sixteen	sixteenth
17 = seventeen	seventeenth
18 = eighteen	eighteenth
19 = nineteen	nineteenth
20 = twenty	twentieth
30 = thirty	thirtieth
40 = forty	fortieth
50 = fifty	fiftieth
60 = sixty	sixtieth
70 = seventy	seventieth
80 = eighty	eightieth
90 = ninety	ninetieth
100 = one hundred	hundredth
1,000 = one thousand	thousandth
1,000,000 = one million	millionth

Mr. George Banks
#17 Cherry Tree Lane
Poppinsville, USA 00000

131
6·0700/0000

date *July 31, 2000*

pay to the order of *Thomson Heinle*   2,184.00

Two thousand one hundred eighty four and 00/100 dollars

MOUNT MONEYBANKS BANK

for *Textbooks*   *Thomson Heinle*

⑈10000000⑈ ⑈0000⑈⑈10000⑈⑈ 0131

Spelling Rules for Verbs and Nouns

Spelling of the -s Form of Verbs and Nouns

Verbs	Nouns	Rule
visit—visit**s** need—need**s** like—like**s** spend—spend**s**	chair—chair**s** bed—bed**s** truck—truck**s** gift—gift**s**	Add **-s** to most words to make the -s form.
mi<u>ss</u>—miss**es** wa<u>sh</u>—wash**es** cat<u>ch</u>—catch**es** fi<u>x</u>—fix**es**	dress—dress**es** dish—dish**es** match—match**es** box—box**es**	Add **-es** to base forms with *ss, sh, ch,* or *x* at the end.
wor<u>ry</u>—worr**ies** t<u>ry</u>—tr**ies** stu<u>dy</u>—stud**ies**	par<u>ty</u>—part**ies** ci<u>ty</u>—cit**ies** ber<u>ry</u>—berr**ies**	If the word ends in a consonant + *y,* change **y** to **-i** and add **-es.**
p<u>ay</u>—pay**s** pl<u>ay</u>—play**s** enj<u>oy</u>—enjoy**s**	b<u>oy</u>—boy**s** d<u>ay</u>—day**s** k<u>ey</u>—key**s**	If the word ends in a vowel + *y,* do not change the -y. Just add **-s.**
	lea<u>f</u>—lea**ves** kni<u>fe</u>—kni**ves**	If the noun ends in *f* or *fe,* change to **ves.**

Irregular -s Forms of Verbs
have—ha**s**
go—go**es**
do—do**es**

Irregular Plural Forms of Nouns	
man—men	foot—feet
woman—women	tooth—teeth
child—children	person—people (or persons)
mouse—mice	fish—fish

Spelling of the *-ing* Forms of Verbs

Verbs	Rule
go—go**ing** eat—eat**ing** spend—spend**ing**	Add **-ing** to most verbs to make the **-ing** form.
tak<u>e</u>—tak**ing** writ<u>e</u>—writ**ing** mak<u>e</u>—mak**ing**	If a verb ends in silent **e**, drop the **e** and add **-ing**. Do NOT double the final consonant. WRONG: writting
pa<u>y</u>—pa**ying** bu<u>y</u>—bu**ying** worr<u>y</u>—worr**ying** stu<u>dy</u>—study**ing**	If a verb ends in a **y**, just add **-ing**. WRONG: studing
s<u>top</u>—sto**pping** <u>run</u>—ru**nning** s<u>pit</u>—spi**tting**	If a one-syllable verb ends in consonant + vowel + consonant, double the final consonant and add **-ing**.
beg<u>ín</u>—begi**nning** perm<u>ít</u>—permi**tting** occ<u>úr</u>—occu**rring**	If a two–syllable word ends in consonant + vowel + consonant, double the final consonant and add **-ing** only if the last syllable is stressed.
ó<u>pen</u>—open**ing** háp<u>pen</u>—happen**ing** devé<u>lop</u>—develop**ing**	If a two or more syllable word ends in consonant + vowel + consonant and the final syllable is not stressed, do NOT double the final consonant. Just add **-ing**.

Spelling of the -*ed* Forms of Regular Past Tense Verbs

Verbs	Rule
listen—listen**ed** look—look**ed**	Add **-ed** to most regular verbs to form the past tense.
ba<u>k</u>e—bake**d** smi<u>l</u>e—smile**d** sa<u>v</u>e—save**d**	If a verb ends in silent **e**, just add **d**. Do NOT double the final consonant. <small>WRONG:</small> smilled
wor<u>r</u>y—wor**ied** stu<u>d</u>y—stud**ied**	If a verb ends in a consonant + **y**, change the **y** to **i** and add **-ed**. <small>WRONG:</small> worryed
enjo<u>y</u>—enjoy**ed** del<u>a</u>y—delay**ed**	If a verb ends in a vowel + **y**, just add **-ed**. <small>WRONG:</small> enjoied
s<u>top</u>—sto**pped** dr<u>ag</u>—dra**gged** sl<u>am</u>—sla**mmed**	If a one-syllable verb ends in consonant + vowel + consonant, double the final consonant and add **-ed**.
per<u>mít</u>—permi**tted** oc<u>cúr</u>—occu**rred**	If a two-syllable word ends in consonant + vowel + consonant, double the final consonant and add **-ed** only if the last syllable is stressed.
ópen—open**ed** háppen— happen**ed** devélop—develop**ed**	If a two or more syllable word ends in consonant + vowel + consonant and the final syllable is not stressed, do NOT double the final consonant. Just add **-ed**.

Spelling of Comparative and Superlative Forms of Adjectives

Simple Adjective	Comparative Adjective	Superlative Adjective	Rule
old cheap	old**er** cheap**er**	old**est** cheap**est**	Add -er and -est to most adjectives.
big hot	bi**gger** ho**tter**	bi**ggest** ho**ttest**	If the adjective ends with consonant-vowel-consonant, double the final consonant before adding -er or -est.
nic<u>e</u> lat<u>e</u>	nicer later	nic**est** lat**est**	If the adjective ends in e, add -r or -st only.
bus<u>y</u> eas<u>y</u>	bus**ier** eas**ier**	bus**iest** eas**iest**	If the adjective ends in y, change y to i and add -er or -est.

Alphabetical List of Irregular Past Forms

Base Form	Past Form	Base Form	Past Form
be	was/were	cut	cut
become	became	do	did
begin	began	draw	drew
bend	bent	drink	drank
bet	bet	drive	drove
bite	bit	eat	ate
blow	blew	fall	fell
break	broke	feed	fed
bring	brought	feel	felt
build	built	fight	fought
buy	bought	find	found
catch	caught	fit	fit
choose	chose	fly	flew
come	came	forget	forgot
cost	cost	get	got

Continued

Base Form	Past Form	Base Form	Past Form
give	gave	run	ran
go	went	say	said
grow	grew	see	saw
have	had	sell	sold
hear	heard	send	sent
hide	hid	shake	shook
hit	hit	shoot	shot
hold	held	shut	shut
hurt	hurt	sing	sang
keep	kept	sit	sat
know	knew	sleep	slept
lead	led	speak	spoke
leave	left	spend	spent
lend	lent	spread	spread
let	let	stand	stood
lie	lay	steal	stole
light	lit (or lighted)	swim	swam
lose	lost	take	took
make	made	teach	taught
mean	meant	tear	tore
meet	met	tell	told
mistake	mistook	think	thought
pay	paid	throw	threw
put	put	understand	understood
quit	quit	wake	woke
read	read	wear	wore
ride	rode	win	won
ring	rang	write	wrote

Capitalization Rules

- The first word in a sentence: **M**y friends are helpful.

- The word "**I**": My sister and **I** took a trip together.

- Names of people: **J**ulia **R**oberts; **G**eorge **W**ashington

- Titles preceding names of people: **D**octor (**D**r.) **S**mith; **P**resident **L**incoln; **Q**ueen **E**lizabeth; **M**r. **R**ogers; **M**rs. **C**arter

- Geographic names: the **U**nited **S**tates; **L**ake **S**uperior; **C**alifornia; the **R**ocky **M**ountains; the **M**ississippi **R**iver

  Note: The word "the" in a geographic name is not capitalized.

- Street names: **P**ennsylvania **A**venue (**A**ve.); **W**all **S**treet (**S**t.); **A**bbey **R**oad (**R**d.)

- Names of organizations, companies, colleges, buildings, stores, hotels: the **R**epublican **P**arty; **H**einle **T**homson; **D**artmouth **C**ollege; the **U**niversity of **W**isconsin; the **W**hite **H**ouse; **B**loomingdale's; the **H**ilton **H**otel

- Nationalities and ethnic groups: **M**exicans; **C**anadians; **S**paniards; **A**mericans; **J**ews; **K**urds; **E**skimos

- Languages: **E**nglish; **S**panish; **P**olish; **V**ietnamese; **R**ussian

- Months: **J**anuary; **F**ebruary

- Days: **S**unday; **M**onday

- Holidays: **C**hristmas; **I**ndependence **D**ay

- Important words in a title: **G**rammar in **C**ontext; **T**he **O**ld **M**an and the **S**ea; **R**omeo and **J**uliet; **T**he **S**ound of **M**usic

  Note: Capitalize "the" as the first word of a title.

Glossary of Grammatical Terms

- **Adjective** An adjective gives a description of a noun.

    It's a *tall* tree.　　He's an *old* man.　　My sisters are *nice*.

- **Adverb** An adverb describes the action of a sentence or an adjective or another adverb.

    She speaks English *fluently*.　　　I drive *carefully*.

    She speaks English *extremely* well.　　She is *very* intelligent.

- **Affirmative** means *yes*.

- **Apostrophe ’** We use the apostrophe for possession and contractions.

    My *sister's* friend is beautiful.　　Today *isn't* Sunday.

- **Article** The definite article is *the*. The indefinite articles are *a* and *an*.

    I have *a* cat.　　I ate *an* apple.　　*The* president was in
    　　　　　　　　　　　　　　　　　　New York last weekend.

- **Base Form** The base form, sometimes called the "simple" form, of the verb has no tense. It has no ending (*-s* or *-ed*): *be, go, eat, take, write*.

    I didn't *go* out.　　　　　　He doesn't *know* the answer.

    You shouldn't *talk* loudly in the library.

- **Capital Letter** A B C D E F G . . .

- **Comma ,**

- **Comparative Form** A comparative form of an adjective or adverb is used to compare two things.

    My house is *bigger* than your house.

    Your car is *better* than my car.

- **Complement** The complement of the sentence is the information after the verb. It completes the verb phrase.

    He works *hard*.　　I slept *for five hours*.　　They are *late*.

- **Consonant** The following letters are consonants: *b, c, d, f, g, h, j, k, l, m, n, p, q, r, s, t, v, w, x, y, z.*

    NOTE: *y* is sometimes considered a vowel, as in the world *syllable*.

- **Contraction** A contraction is made up of two words put together with an apostrophe.

    He's my brother.　*You're* late.　　They *won't* talk to me.

    (*He's = he is*)　　(*You're = you are*)　　(*won't = will not*)

- **Count Noun** Count nouns are nouns that we can count. They have a singular and a plural form.

  1 pen — 3 pens   1 table — 4 tables

- **Frequency Words** Frequency words are *always, usually, often, sometimes, rarely, seldom, never.*

  I *never* drink coffee.   We *always* do our homework.

- **Imperative** An imperative sentence gives a command or instructions. An imperative sentence omits the word *you*.

  Come here.   *Don't be* late.   Please *sit* down.

- **Infinitive** An infinitive is *to* + base form.

  I want *to leave.*   You need *to be* here on time.

- **Modal** The modal verbs are *can, could, shall, should, will, would, may, might, must.*

  They *should* leave.   I *must* go.

- **Negative** means no.

- **Nonaction Verb** A nonaction verb has no action. We do not use a continuous tense (*be* + verb *-ing*) with a nonaction verb. The nonaction verbs are: *believe, cost, care, have, hear, know, like, love, matter, mean, need, own, prefer, remember, see, seem, think, understand, want.*

  She *has* a computer.   We *love* our mother.

- **Noncount Noun** A noncount noun is a noun that we don't count. It has no plural form.

  She drank some *water.*   He ate some *rice.*
  I need *money.*

- **Noun** A noun is a person (*brother*), a place (*kitchen*), or a thing (*table*). Nouns can be either count (*1 table, 2 tables*) or noncount (*money, water*).

  My *brother* lives in California.   My *sisters* live in New York.
  I get *mail* from them.

- **Object** The object of the sentence follows the verb. It receives the action of the verb.

  He bought *a car.*   I saw *a movie.*   I met *your brother.*

- **Object Pronoun** Use object pronouns (*me, you, him, her, it, us, them*) after the verb or preposition.

  He likes *her.*   I saw the movie. Let's talk about *it.*

- **Parentheses ( )**

- **Participle, Present** The present participle is verb + *-ing*.

  She is *sleeping.*   They were *laughing.*

- **Period** .

- **Phrase** A group of words that go together.

    Last month my sister came to visit.

    There is a strange car *in front of my house.*

- **Plural** Plural means more than one. A plural noun usually ends with *-s*.

    She has beautiful *eyes.*

- **Possessive Form** Possessive forms show ownership or relationship.

    Mary's coat is in the closet.   *My* brother lives in Miami.

- **Preposition** A preposition is a connecting word: *about, above, across, after, around, as, at, away, before, behind, below, by, down, for, from, in, into, like, of, off, on, out, over, to, under, up, with.*

    The book is *on* the table.

- **Pronoun** A pronoun takes the place of a noun.

    I have a new car. I bought *it* last week.

    John likes Mary, but *she* doesn't like *him.*

- **Punctuation** Period . Comma , Colon : Semicolon ; Question Mark ? Exclamation Mark !

- **Question Mark** ?

- **Regular Verb** A regular verb forms its past tense with *-ed.*

    He *worked* yesterday.   We *listened* to the radio.

- ***s* Form** A present tense verb that ends in *-s* or *-es.*

    He *lives* in New York.   She *watches* TV a lot.

- **Sentence** A sentence is a group of words that contains a subject[1] and a verb (at least) and gives a complete thought.

    SENTENCE: She came home.

    NOT A SENTENCE: When she came home

- **Simple Form of Verb** The simple form of the verb, also called the "base" form, has no tense; it never has an *-s, -ed,* or *-ing* ending.

    Did you *see* the movie?   I can't *find* his phone number.

- **Singular** Singular means one.

    She ate a *sandwich.*   I have one *television.*

- **Subject** The subject of the sentence tells who or what the sentence is about.

    My sister bought a new car. *The car* is beautiful.

---

[1] In an imperative sentence, the subject *you* is omitted: *Sit down. Come here.*

- **Subject Pronouns** Use subject pronouns (*I, you, he, she, it, we, you, they*) before a verb.

    They speak Japanese.   *We* speak Spanish.

- **Superlative Form** A superlative form of an adjective shows the number one item in a group of three or more.

    January is the *coldest* month of the year.

    You have the *best* seat in the room.

- **Syllable** A syllable is a part of a word that has only one vowel sound. (Some words have only one syllable.)

    change (one syllable)   after (af·ter = 2 syllables)

    look (one syllable)   responsible (re·spon·si·ble = 4 syllables)

- **Tense** A verb has tense. Tense shows when the action of the sentence happened.

    SIMPLE PRESENT: She usually *works* hard.

    FUTURE: She *will work* tomorrow.

    PRESENT CONTINUOUS: She *is working* now.

    SIMPLE PAST: She *worked* yesterday.

- **Verb** A verb is the action of the sentence.

    He *runs* fast.   I *speak* English.

- **Vowel** The following letters are vowels: *a, e, i, o, u. Y* is sometimes considered a vowel (for example, in the word *syllable*).

The United States of America: Major Cities

The United States of America

AL Alabama	HI Hawaii	MA Massachusetts	NM New Mexico	SD South Dakota
AK Alaska	ID Idaho	MI Michigan	NY New York	TN Tennessee
AZ Arizona	IL Illinois	MN Minnesota	NC North Carolina	TX Texas
AR Arkansas	IN Indiana	MS Mississippi	ND North Dakota	UT Utah
CA California	IA Iowa	MO Missouri	OH Ohio	VT Vermont
CO Colorado	KS Kansas	MT Montana	OK Oklahoma	VA Virginia
CT Connecticut	KY Kentucky	NE Nebraska	OR Oregon	WA Washington
DE Delaware	LA Louisiana	NV Nevada	PA Pennsylvania	WV West Virginia
FL Florida	ME Maine	NH New Hampshire	RI Rhode Island	WI Wisconsin
GA Georgia	MD Maryland	NJ New Jersey	SC South Carolina	WY Wyoming
				DC* District of Columbia

*The District of Columbia is not a state. Washington, D.C. is the capital of the United States.
Note: Washinton, D.C., and Washington state are not the same.

Index